Profile
of
William Carlos Williams

Compiled by

Jerome Mazzaro

State University of New York at Buffalo

Charles E. Merrill Publishing Company
A Bell & Howell Company
Columbus, Ohio

CHARLES E. MERRILL PROFILES

Under the Editorship of
Matthew J. Bruccoli and Joseph Katz

The author and publisher gratefully acknowledge the following for permission to quote:
From William Carlos Williams, *Collected Earlier Poems*, Copyright 1938 by William Carlos Williams. *Paterson I-IV*, Copyright 1946, 1951 by William Carlos Williams. *Pictures from Brueghel*, © 1962 by William Carlos Williams. *Collected Later Poems*, Copyright 1944 by William Carlos Williams. Reprinted by permission of New Directions Publishing Corporation and Laurence Pollinger Limited.

ISBN: 0-675-09198-5

Library of Congress Catalog Card Number: 79-152710

1 2 3 4 5 6 7—77 76 75 74 73 72 71

Printed in the United States of America

Preface

In 1946, William Carlos Williams wrote to an Australian editor that he stood against the notion of Ezra Pound that mind "fertilizes mind, that the mere environment is just putty," and that man "since Joyce discovered Hamlet, is out to seek his own father—his spiritual father, that is." Instead, he proposed "that there may be another literary source continuing the greatness of the past which does not develop androgynetically from the past itself mind to mind but from the present, from the hurley-burley of political encounters which determine or may determine it, direct." He went on to note, "We must acknowledge to ourselves that the origin of the new *is* society, that each society not only originates but fertilizes its whole life, of a piece. . . . If a man in his fatuous dreams cuts himself off from that supplying female [society], he dries up his sources—as Pound did in the end heading straight for literary sterility." Earlier in *Paterson I* (1946), Williams had prepared for these statements by making the city Paterson the female source of the writer's inspiration. By *Paterson III* (1948), the writer could no longer be differentiated from his work: "nothing is so unclear, between man and / his writing, as to which is the man and / which the thing and of them both which / is the more to be valued." This same continuous flow from society to man to writing has suggested the organizational pattern for this collection which begins with a survey of the Williams foreground—that flurry of literary activity and experimentation during the Tens and Twenties—and then moves to his early writings and personality before settling more exclusively into these writings, their techniques and their theories.

iii

The collection closes with Hugh Kenner's eloquent tribute for this man who in *Kora in Hell* (1920) had depicted the relationship between art and life as "following now the words, *allegro,* now the contrary beat of the glossy leg" and language within a poem in *Many Loves* (1942) as "the drama of words—words in love, / hot words, copulating, drinking, running, / bleeding!" It is Williams who, at one point in the *Autobiography* (1951), describes how "in illness, in the permission I as a physician have had to be present at deaths and births, at the tormented battles between daughter and diabolic mother, shattered by a gone brain—just there—for a split second—from one side or the other, it has fluttered before me for a moment, a phrase which I quickly write down on anything at hand, any piece of paper I can grab." This poet, physician, blunt craftsman was born in Rutherford, New Jersey, on September 17, 1883. He attended preparatory schools in the United States and abroad before enrolling in a medical program at the University of Pennsylvania. There he became friendly with a young Drexel art student, Charles Demuth, as well as Pound and Hilda Doolittle. After graduation he spent more time in Europe before returning to Rutherford in 1910 to begin his medical practice, marry, and produce in addition to the over 2,000 babies he delivered more than twenty-five volumes of fiction, criticism, and poetry.

His longest major poem, *Paterson*, appeared in five volumes between 1946 and 1958, but both before and after its appearance Williams enjoyed a distinguished reputation as a fine lyric poet and a leader of *avant-garde* poetics. In 1926, he received the Dial Award for Services to American Literature, but his major awards came later. In 1949, he received the National Book Award for *Paterson III* and *The Selected Poems*. A Pulitzer Prize was awarded to him posthumously in 1963 for *Pictures from Brueghel and Other Poems*. I have tried in this volume to reduce as much as possible any overlap with John Engels's *Studies in "Paterson"* (1971) and J. Hillis Miller's *William Carlos Williams: A Collection of Critical Essays* (1966) and, with the exception of Randall Jarrell's criticism, to restrict myself to material not available in book form. I feel that the Jarrell pieces raise objections to Williams's writing that all serious readers must either refute or face squarely. Philip L. Gerber's "So Much Depends: The Williams Foreground" makes its first appearance here.

                                                                                J.M.

Contents

Contents

Chronicle of Events

1883   William Carlos Williams born on September 17, Rutherford, New Jersey, the son of William George and Raquel Hélène Hoheb Williams.

1897–1899   In school in Switzerland and later briefly in Paris.

1902   Graduated Horace Mann High School.

1902–1906   Student at the Medical School of the University of Pennsylvania. While completing his M.D. there, meets Ezra Pound, Hilda Doolittle, and the painter, Charles Demuth.

1906–1909   Internships at the old French Hospital and at Child's Hospital in New York City.

1909   *Poems* privately printed. Returns to Europe to study pediatrics at Leipzig and to visit his brother in Rome and Ezra Pound in London.

1910   Begins medical practice in Rutherford.

1912   Marries Florence Herman.

1913   *The Tempers* published in London.

1914–1919   Poems published in Ezra Pound's *Des Imagistes* anthology. Encounters poets of the *Others* movement, including Marianne Moore and Wallace Stevens.

1917   Publishes *Al Que Quiere!*

1920   Publishes *Kora in Hell: Improvisations.*

1920–1923   Edits *Contact* with Robert McAlmon. Publishes *Sour Grapes*; *Spring and All*; *The Great American Novel*; and *Go Go.*

1924   Travels in Europe with wife.

1925   Publishes *In the American Grain.*

1926   Dial Award for excellence in writing.

1928   Publishes *A Voyage to Pagany,* based on his 1924 trip.

1929   Publishes a translation of Philippe Soupault's *Last Nights of Paris.*

1931   Guarantor's Prize from *Poetry.*

1932   Publishes *The Cod Head; A Novelette and Other Prose;* and *The Knife of the Times and Other Stories.*

1934   Publishes *Collected Poems 1921–1931.*

1937–1938   Publishes *White Mule; Life Along the Passaic River;* and *The Complete Collected Poems.*

1940–1945   Publishes *In the Money* (Part II of *White Mule*); *The Broken Span; Trial Horse No. 1* (retitled *Many Loves*); and *The Wedge.*

1946   Publishes *Paterson, Book One.*

1947   Lectures at the University of Washington (returns in 1950).

1948–1949   Publishes *Paterson, Book Two; A Dream of Love; The Clouds; The Pink Church; Selected Poems;* and *Paterson, Book Three.* Made a Fellow of the Library of Congress.

1950   National Book Award for *Selected Poems* and *Paterson, Book Three.* Publishes *Make Light of It: Collected Stories,* and *The Collected Later Poems.*

1951   Publishes *The Collected Earlier Poems; Paterson, Book Four;* and *Autobiography.* Suffers first stroke and retires from medical practice.

1952   Publishes *The Build-Up,* the last of the *White Mule* trilogy. Appointed Consultant in Poetry to the Library of Congress.

1953   Bollingen Award for excellence in contemporary verse.

1954   Publishes *The Desert Music and Other Poems*; *Selected Essays*; and a translation in collaboration with his mother of Don Francisco de Quevedo's *A Dog and the Fever*.

1955   Embarks on a reading tour of colleges across the country.

1955–1962   Publishes *Journey to Love*; *The Selected Letters*; *Paterson, Book Five*; *I Wanted to Write a Poem*; *Yes, Mrs. Williams: A Personal Record of My Mother*; *The Farmers' Daughters*; *Many Loves and Other Plays*; and *Pictures from Brueghel and Other Poems*.

1963   Dies on March 4. Awarded Pulitzer Prize for *Pictures from Brueghel* posthumously in May.

Philip L. Gerber

So Much Depends:
The Williams Foreground

The Age Demanded

"He was," Randall Jarrell noted in "A View of Three Poets" (1951), "the last of the good poets of his generation to become properly appreciated." Perhaps the greater marvel is that William Carlos Williams was appreciated at all: that he was empowered to become the poet he did, produce the body of work he did, to merit appreciation. He was not a born trailblazer, needing to be shown the way, sometimes even then not seeing rapidly. He was not ready to die for art; important as expression was to him, it took a second priority to earning a living, and the pediatric career he followed consumed his energies day and night. He was born into a poetic wasteland unconducive to experimentation and hostile to the new, an era in which even the battling revolutionary seemed doomed.

Consider the facts. The household words of nineteenth-century verse had been the popular three-name poets, all, from Bryant to Lowell, born prior to 1820. Their British-flavored establishment was sufficiently ironclad to dissuade any challengers, from the first quarter of the century until the last, no poet of major stature arising as a genuine threat. And as the three-namers lived habitually into their eighties, when the last leaf on the tree, Holmes, let go in 1894, their tradition was all but canonized. With Whitman discredited (so far as possible) and Dickinson unknown

—and both dead—America for all intents and purposes was left a land without poets. Of those born late enough possibly to break the fetters, William Vaughn Moody inched forward all too cautiously, and Crane died too young. Robinson's efforts were ignored. Those who would eventually compose a new thrust (Frost, Masters, Lindsay, Sandburg, Pound) were as yet either silent or conformist. Looking back, William Stanley Braithwaite observed in his *Anthology of Magazine Verse for 1914* (1914): "From 1900 to 1905 poetry had declined; and I think there has never been another period in our history when so unintelligent and indifferent an attitude existed toward the art." The age demanded an image in the mirror-likeness of what had gone before—"beautiful," safe, and empty—and it got overwhelmingly what it ordered.

How then account for Williams? To be sure, his own personality was good soil. There was in him that native rebelliousness, much of which, in terms of verse, stemmed from Whitman, the poet with whom he is most often—and correctly—linked. Robert Lowell, for example, in his appreciation, "William Carlos Williams" (1961), asserts, "*Paterson* is our *Leaves of Grass*," and Jarrell, in his Introduction to *The Selected Poems of William Carlos Williams* (1949), claims, "The hair-raising originality of some of Whitman's language is another bond between the two." His Whitmanesque qualities are readily apparent: the radical experimentation in form, language, and subject; the exuberant tone, at times verging on bombast; the affinity for the oracular, seen especially in "public" poems exhorting his townspeople ("Tract," etc.). In his criticism the mature Williams at times paraphrases Whitman in language startlingly reminiscent: "The mark of a great poet is the extent to which he is aware of his time and NOT, unless I be a fool, the weight of loveliness in his meters."[1] But the Whitman strain was unapparent in the youthful Williams, submerged, suppressed, locked out. His early Whitmanesque scribbling—eighteen thick notebooks!—he kept packed away like a secret diary, parading for other eyes only his imitation Keats.

There was also an inborn desire to achieve; that was in his favor, a wholesome sign, but again no assurance of meritorious

[1]"Belly Music," *Others,* V (July 1919), 27; hereafter referred to as BM and page number. The abbreviations for the other Williams' works which have been used are as follows: A—*The Autobiography of William Carlos Williams* (New York, 1951); SL—*The Selected Letters of William Carlos Williams,* ed. John C. Thirlwall (New York, 1957); IWWP—*I Wanted to Write a Poem,* ed. Edith Heal (Boston, 1958); CEP—*The Collected Earlier Poems* (New York, 1951).

performance. Williams' first poem was, he says, "born like a bolt
out of the blue" when he was perhaps seventeen and in the grip
of near-suicidal adolescent disillusionment. He recounts it in his
autobiography, and if he is quoting from a script and not from
wishful thinking, the verse, much like a fragment from Crane, is a
good deal better than much of what he wrote in the next ten
years:

> A black, black cloud
> flew over the sun
> driven by fierce flying
> rain.

Seeing what he had wrought, he was engulfed with joy: "From
that moment I was a poet" (A, 47).

Not quite; for between desire and art too often falls the shadow. It took twenty years to shake him loose, formed, full, and
ripe, from the limb of the past. His inherent traits needed that
time to assert themselves fully; he needed to feed long on for-
mative influences before his own independent growth took place.
In early life, his first great stroke of luck was falling in with the
right friends. In 1902 he went to Philadelphia in search of a
medical education and found Pound and Hilda Doolittle. Both
remained life long friends, and Pound particularly could be re-
lied upon to mudge one along with him into the vanguard, pushing or tugging if that be essential. Yet even the great Ezra's
influence did not prevent his friend's first published verses
(*Poems*, 1909) from taking shape in the most dismally "accept-
able" manner:

> I've found anticipation of a day
> O'erfilled with pure diversion presently,
> For I must read a lady poesie
> The while we glide by many a leafy bay.[2]

For balance, it should be acknowledged in all justice that the
apprentice poems of a host of other newcomers (the early work
of Frost, etc.) were little different and no better.

To excel was his ambition. He had to be the best. He was filled
with "eager desires, which no world, and certainly not the Ruther-

---

[2]John C. Thirlwall, ed., "The Lost Poems of William Carlos Williams,"
in *New Directions 16* (New York, 1957), p. 5.

ford of those days, could satisfy. . . . I was gnawing my insides all day long" (SL, 80). Given his choice, he would have striven for stardom in athletics, a first love dashed by overexertion. Unable to see "anything worth striving for save greatness" (BM, 27), he turned to art, and might easily have developed as a painter, for he was accustomed from boyhood to seeing canvas and paint around the house, reminders of his mother's years in Paris, where her student work had been awarded three medals in painting. Occasionally he appropriated her palette and old tubes to dabble for himself. But poetry, with its linguistic medium, appealed to him finally as the more articulate art, and the natural acuteness of physical sensation, the leaping joy in the act of living, which had been at the heart of his "mad athletic excesses," could serve the painter and the writer equally well, so that ultimately these qualities blossomed as a foremost virtue of his poetry. He reveled in the landscape, colors of violets, stars of Bethlehem, geraniums, anemones, hepaticas, all abounding near Rutherford; the deep blue of grape hyacinths were the highlight of a country walk with Hilda Doolittle in Pennsylvania; and the "astonishing" sight of blossoms like huge yellow and green tulips on a tree. All these glories, he recollected, "were as much a part of my expanding existence as breathing" (A, 20).

Explosion in a Shingle Factory

Williams' interest in, receptiveness to painting served him well when he encountered the first of the major early twentieth-century revolutions that shaped his young manhood, for the revolution in the visual arts preceded that in verse. The overthrow in Europe of the old order by Matisse, Cézanne, Braque, Picasso—and before them the impressionists—soon spread to America. Again, Williams was in luck. At Penn he had chummed with Charles Demuth, a Drexel student who, studying art in Paris in 1907, broke with the naturalistic school to follow the new cubism. Living as he did within commuting distance from Greenwich Village, Williams was able to see a good deal of Demuth, and through him to discern the new concepts, revelatory to one who was above all impressionable and, as Wallace Stevens noticed, "interested in anything new that might be going around."[3]

---

[3]*Letters of Wallace Stevens,* ed. Holly Stevens (New York, 1966), p. 768.

Demuth himself was shaping strange, intriguing cubist pieces, architectural landscapes that bulged with factories and machines, laced with intersecting diagonals in contrasting shafts of light and dark. Conrad Aiken's observation in *Scepticisms* (1919) is uncannily suggestive of the influence derived from Demuth's canvases: "We get the impression from [Williams'] poems that his world is a world of plane surfaces, bizarrely coloured, and cunningly arranged so as to get an effect of depth and solidity; but we do not get depth itself." The artist's "poster portrait" of his friend Williams is representative: numbers, letters, broken words, a brilliance of red and gold, and the title "I Saw the Figure 5 in Gold" taken from a Williams poem.

Andrew Ritchie's summation in *Charles Demuth* (1950), "In the first flood of mature work, at the age of thirty-two, Demuth definitely 'arrives' as an artist. The intervening years between 1907 and 1915 were spent assimilating much that was to be learned from the *avant garde* in Paris, both as to expressionistic freedom of color and cubist analysis of form," would require little revision to describe Williams' career quite accurately. Through Demuth, Williams was familiarized with the work of radical painters as well as with Alfred Steiglitz, the father-surrogate who sponsored them all at his 291 Fifth Avenue galleries, and who was himself performing comparable experiments in the field of photography. Steiglitz in 1909 backed the first public showing for another Williams friend, Marsden Hartley, who had broken dramatically with academic technique when he laid his pigment areas in an unconventional Segantini "stitch," side by side, in deep impasto, rather than blending his colors for the usual literal, photographic effect. In process of developing his own bold style, he absorbed the inspiration of Picasso, whose early cubist paintings he aped, of Cézanne, and particularly of the great colorist Kandinsky. Hartley, who habituated the evening gatherings to which young Dr. Williams hurried via ferry after his day's practice closed, was unique in being a writer also, at times scribbling *vers libre* on the backs of canvases. His inherited money enabled him to reserve scheduled portions of each year, first for the one art, then the other. The same little magazines that welcomed Williams published Hartley as well, and in June, 1918, the two appeared together in *Poetry*, Hartley given the lead position with a group of poems, Williams contributing "Le Médecin Malgré Lui." The pair appeared together at least twice in *The Little*

Review, and Hartley contributed to *Others* while Williams was connected with it. For his paintings of the 1911–1913 period, Hartley employed the label "improvisations," and Williams may have had this in mind when he used the identical term a few years later for his *Kora in Hell* pieces.

A third painter to influence Williams (Charles Sheeler was a fourth but arrived later) was the abstractionist Stuart Davis, whose career, as described in Rudi Blesh's *Stuart Davis* (1960), is again strongly suggestive of Williams, simultaneously sweating his way from "Postlude" to "Tract": "The paintings of these years [1913–1918] are like pages in a diary, recording his struggle toward a personal, modern style." As he approached his distinctive style, Davis abandoned completely painting from nature as the academy had taught and insisted upon. Yet he did not abandon nature itself, but trained himself to the habit of conceptual rather than optical perspective. In his studio he fused into a single focus drawings of different places and objects, not excepting such "found" items as the ubiquitous gasoline pumps and boldly lettered signs that lent his work a strong effect of chance. When Williams was in process of completing *Kora in Hell,* that seemingly arbitrary, haphazard compendium of disparate prose and verse, it was to Davis' "mental collages" that he, quite logically and with infallible intuition, went for a frontispiece. Despite not having met the painter, "Floss and I went to Gloucester and got permission from Stuart Davis to use his art—an impressionistic view of the simultaneous." Davis' *Multiple Views,* composed of closely-packed vignettes occupying a surface plane and abandoning any attempt at deep space, "was, graphically, exactly what I was trying to do in words" (IWWP, 29).

What could better demonstrate the intimate ties linking the visual and literary experiments of the era? Via two media the same striving, with similar results. Blesh describes Davis' rapid capturing of scenes and interpolated vignettes as being "like quick flashes of seeing that are also flashes of memory," an insight hardly half a step from Kenneth Burke's depiction of Williams in "Heaven's First Law" (1922) as "the master of the glimpse . . . . there is the eye, and there is the thing upon which that eye alights; while the relationship existing between the two is a poem." Finally, Davis' work is said by Blesh to possess "a kind of literary quality in visual terms, shifts of scene that are also shifts in time and mood, a kind of stream-of-consciousness technique in graphic symbols."

Hartley was occupied abroad, but Davis and Demuth both exhibited in the 1913 Armory Show, that bomb that blew the academic tradition to smithereens. Davis exhibited five watercolors and, upon viewing the show, told himself, "That settled it. I would be a modern artist." It is not difficult to hear Williams, upon witnessing the explosion of New Poetry between 1910 and 1913, telling himself precisely this. He also was "on exhibit" at the Armory Show. Invited to read his "Overture to a Dance of Locomotives," he did so, although not all the ladies in the audience remained to hear its conclusion. The poem presages much of Williams' work and is important principally in providing early evidence of what he had learned from his painter friends; the use of native materials found close at hand (he must be the first since Whitman to address a poem to a locomotive); a visual snaring of objects, snapshot-clear and in bold primary color: "earth-colored walls of bare limestone / . . . Porters in red hats run on narrow platforms" (CEP, 194); but above all, the effort's vignetted organization (or unorganization), a scheme of movement that would distinguish his more characteristic efforts. It is not surprising that commentators, scurrying for the appropriate words to describe Williams' technique, invariably arrive at terms appropriated from the visual arts: collage; mosaic; or Stevens' choice, "mobile-like."[4]

Williams himself, describing a poem as a "machine made of words," may have had in mind the mechanisms that crammed the modern canvases of Demuth, Léger, Davis and so many others, but, in any event, was utilizing a new, contemporary, and unmistakably American concept; no one else could describe a poem in this way, just as no one but an American would call a home a machine for living. Searching for an explanation of the arbitrary, "chance" quality of Davis' work, Blesh notes that nothing like it occurs in art of previous ages, concluding that we "might chance upon it altogether by accident, glancing at two successive frames of a motion picture film." The motion picture seems at last the secret, for the technique adopted by Davis—and then by Williams—is at heart cinematic (and therefore machine), the motion picture camera being constructed precisely to produce the movement, the lapses, the simultaneity, the abrupt shifts of scene, the "glimpses" and juxtapositions which Williams' poems increasingly achieved. Without strain one can read "Overture to a Dance

---

[4]*Ibid.*, p. 801.

of Locomotives" as a scenario; the entire poem opens when approached from this stance, as does much of Williams' work from this point on.

Risorgimento

In August 1912, Pound, writing from London to assure Harriet Monroe in Chicago that her impending magazine, *Poetry: A Magazine of Verse*, would be his exclusive outlet in America, expressed his faith in "our American Risorgimento" and added: "that awakening will make the Italian Renaissance look like a tempest in a teapot."[5] As usual, his exuberance carried him away somewhat, but soon after 1912 the renaissance in poetry was fully underway. Literature being what it is and not assimilable in a gallery display, it lacked the bomblike impact of the Armory Show, which during four weeks was viewed by 800,000 people. The revival of poetry swept in more like a great wave, with its own solid, leisurely force. If any single event might be cited as formally launching this risorgimento, it would occur on September 23, when, after a two-year campaign of begging and bribing and dogged effort, Miss Monroe produced *Poetry's* first issue. It was not a spectacular number: Grace Hazard Conkling, some previously unseen William Vaughn Moody—but it did contain Pound's "To Whistler" and "Middle-aged," and more important, Pound, who had agreed to become "foreign correspondent," was already at work rounding up the work of Richard Aldington, expatriate H.D., and others, plus contributions from Rabindranath Tagore, at this point unknown and unpublished in America although on the verge of a Nobel Prize. Eventually he would snare his major catch, Eliot's "Prufrock," the first lines of which Miss Monroe said "nearly took our breath away,"[6] and would begin in *Poetry's* pages the serialization of his own first *Cantos*. In America, the poets—many of them struggling along their own lines without much hope of acceptance, let alone recognition—began to comprehend that a voice was available at last; and in the wings of the stage *Poetry* provided, an amazing cast of future stars was congregating, of which Sandburg and Lindsay would be among the first to debut.

Trailing by a few weeks the inauguration of *Poetry* came Fer-

---

[5]Harriet Monroe, *A Poet's Life* (New York, 1938), p. 260.
[6]*Ibid.*, p. 394.

dinand Earle's *The Lyric Year*, proposed as an annual prize anthology. Earle's call for contest poems—a healthy $500.00 for first prize—had inspired a flood of manuscripts which required judges to read beside a pair of capacious wastebaskets for the spillover of "insipid and drivelling nonsense"[7] which 10,000 entries inevitably produced. One hundred "best" poems were published, many by names soon to be familiar: Zoë Akins, William Rose Benet, Witter Bynner, Donn Byrne, Arthur Davison Ficke, Joyce Kilmer, Vachel Lindsay, James Oppenheim, Sara Teasdale, Louis Untermeyer, John Hall Wheelock. The prizewinner was Orrick Johns, whose *Asphalt* would be an important volume in 1917. Second place went to the Californian George Sterling, and third to Ridgely Torrence. Today *The Lyric Year* is known for its inclusion of the poem Earle had backed for first prize but which failed to rate high enough otherwise to place higher than fourth: Edna St. Vincent Millay's "Renascence."

Miss Millay, a prodigy of scarcely eighteen when she wrote her poem, was unique; the outburst of poetry becomes more explicable by realizing that in 1912 Robinson and Masters were already forty-three; Amy Lowell thirty-eight; Frost thirty-seven; Sandburg thirty-four; Lindsay and Stevens thirty-three; Sara Teasdale twenty-eight; and Pound twenty-seven, with Marianne Moore and T. S. Eliot relative youngsters at twenty-five and twenty-four respectively. Obviously there existed, although unknown and unsung, a readymade cadre of mature poets. Masters was in the midst of a law career and had published pseudonymously, Amy Lowell had been experimenting in private for a decade; Frost, who had written his "Death of the Hired Man" as early as 1905, had given up on America and sailed to seek a publisher in London. Sandburg worked a reporter's beat; Lindsay was tramping through Kansas, trading rhymes for bread; Stevens was comfortably ensconced in his insurance office. None of these could so much as claim poetry as a chief occupation, yet all of them were ready, their foregrounds complete, and waited only to be unleashed.

In this company Williams (twenty-nine in 1912) stood midway in age between the eldest, Robinson, and the youngest, Cummings, then eighteen. Typically, he also had entered a professional career, restricting his writing necessarily to spare moments, learn-

---

[7]Earle as quoted by Allan Ross Macdougall in *Letters of Edna St. Vincent Millay* (New York, 1952), p. 17.

ing whatever he could along the way. Early in 1913, when *Poetry* had run for only a few issues, he mailed Miss Monroe a group of six poems: "Sicilian Immigrant's Song," "Peace on Earth," "Proof of Immortality," "Postlude," "The Portent," and "Madonna Mia." The last two were returned, but the others appeared in the magazine's June number. It was Williams' first magazine publication in America—another "discovery" for *Poetry*.

There was nothing in these verses to take one's breath away, and little evidence of a revolutionary mind; their chief characteristic was their conventionality. "The Portent," rejected, comes actually a good league closer to the eventual Williams than does the accepted "Proof of Immortality" with its more stilted diction—"And thou, beloved, art that godly thing!"—and Williams collected it in *The Tempers* (1913) while dumping "Immortality." Most advanced of all is the verse Miss Monroe preferred, "Sicilian Immigrant's Song," a "talk-poem" attempting to capture the reaction of an Italian torn from the blue sea and flaring sun, the orange and fig of his Palermo and deposited in the chill grey harbor of New York. Unlike its fellow poems, it reaches for an immediate idiom: "O—eh—li! La—la! / Donna! Donna!" In this sense it is a major advance beyond the Hellenistic focus (echoes of H.D., unnatural to Williams) that mars "Postlude":

> Ripples at Philae, in and out,
> And lips, my Lesbian . . . .
> Your hair is my Carthage.   (CEP, 16)

Yet in the following year (1914) when Pound chose to boost Williams in his slim little anthology, *Des Imagistes*, it was "Postlude" that he included; he also was inordinately fond of things Greek. Soon imagism was on its way to becoming a rallying center for the New Poetry and Williams, who in his first contributor's note in *Poetry* had been described merely as a New York area resident and medical practitioner, was upon his second appearance labeled categorically "a prominent American member of the imagist group."[8] He was not, of course, and to Miss Monroe's credit she later recognized that "no group could hold" this "restive"[9] individual.

---

[8]*Poetry*, VI (May 1915), 105.
[9]Monroe, p. 269.

"My Absolute Egoism"

Restive—a fine, explicit adjective for the Williams of the 'teens.
Something momentous was underway, and he, although thirty
years old, stood on no more than the fringe, something of an
attendant lord, a position which any great natural competitor
would find untenable. "Around 1914 I began to know other poets"
(IWWP, 19), he reminisced in his later years. He knew them first
by example, in the new periodicals and then through their celebrated books: Lindsay, with *General Booth*, then *The Congo* and
Chinese Nightingale; Masters with his phenomenally bestselling
Spoon River; Eliot and *Prufrock*; Sandburg and *Chicago, Smoke
and Steel, Cornhuskers*; Frost home from England with *A Boy's
Will* already in print, and almost at once *North of Boston*, another
bestseller and one of the most consistently outstanding collections
ever published in America. Amy Lowell, her decade of preparation
behind her, took flame from Pound, asserted imperiously her personal claim to leadership of the Imagists, and poured out volume
after volume; her "Patterns" became an anthology staple over-
night. Edna Millay, nearly ten years Williams' junior, released
her first collection and was acclaimed America's lyricist par excellence. Poetry most definitely was on the move now, major poets
and minor all writing, and *publishing*, most of it *vers libre*,
experimental in a dozen directions at once. The brothers Benet
were scarcely out of college and already producing volumes to high
praise; Stevens, reluctant to collect, but noted as the author of
"Peter Quince" and "Sunday Morning." Democratizing art, the
anthologists entered the field: Braithwaite and his annual collections of verse from magazines; Untermeyer beginning a career as
an anthologist which would continue for more than fifty years; in
1917 the king of them all, *The New Poetry*, edited by Harriet
Monroe herself.

With all this hubbub, Williams was in full accord, having arrived
long since at his commitment: "Nothing is good save the new."[10]
"I wanted a new order. I was positively repelled by the old order
which, to me, amounted to restriction" (IWWP, 18). But what
had he, personally, done to bring about this new order? There
were his two volumes of poems, both privately printed at his own
expense, while Houghton Mifflin, Macmillan, and Holt were com-

---

[10]"Prologue II," *The Little Review*, VI (May 1919), 74.

peting for the big names, and his second volume, *The Tempers*, boasted no more than a miniscule advance over his first. Pound, his college chum, at a loss for words in an introductory note for it, could honestly say no more than "Mr. Williams may write some very good poetry," and attempt to salve the sting by adding, "It's not every one of whom one can say that" (IWWP, 12). At least two poems, "Hic Jacet" and "To Wish Myself Courage" showed promise of new directions, but it was clear that what new work Williams presented was not yet new enough. In 1914, compared with the radical departures in subject, form, and language made by Lindsay, Sandburg, and others in the vanguard, his achievement seemed the acme of convention. He was "always conscious of being late" (IWWP, 34), of having begun the race under a handicap of age, and this, combined with his strong drive, could produce intolerance. At times he was irascible. As late as 1919 he continued to rail against the cult of youth: "The devil with youth! What does youth care or what do I care for it? What significance has youth? . . . It is damnable nonsense to think to anchor a poet on his Byronic adolescence of body and mind or to think to grant him only the province of cynicism. I began when I was twenty. I BEGAN THEN. OTHERS saw its inception when I was thirty, when I had already proved a failure time after time" (BM, 28, 32).

The spectacle of indisputable achievements by his fellow poets could be depressing, even discouraging, yet to one of Williams' temperament it could also be a tremendous spur. To catch up, to keep up, perhaps to overtake, he must learn, and quickly. A good deal was being absorbed, through his pores, covertly as it were, and undoubtedly without conscious notion of how it might soon crop up in his verses, and now he began to throw himself into as full a participation in the renaissance as his practice would permit. A new possibility opened in 1914 with the inception of *The Little Review*, and Williams, accepted for its pages from the beginning, was forever in the debt of its editor, Margaret Anderson, always in his damnation of critics and editors excepting her as "the only one of them who gets up a magazine which is not a ragbag" (BM, 27). *Others*, under the aegis of friend Alfred Kreymborg, went into print in 1915, and Williams felt "a strange quickening of artistic life" in New York. "Actually," he wrote *The Egoist*, "it seemed that the weight of centuries was about to be lifted. One could actually get a poem published without having to think of anything except that it be good artistically" (SL, 30, 31). Because the

Others offices were close at hand, it was possible for Williams to play an active role in its affairs, not only contributing his verse but sharing responsibility as editor and meeting in the process a number of those whose worship of art matched his own: Orrick Johns, the *Lyric Year* winner; Malcolm Cowley; Man Ray, the photographer; Helen Hoyt, Walter Arensberg, and Mina Loy; red-haired Marianne Moore; Maxwell Bodenheim; Lola Ridge, whose *The Ghetto* won high praise in 1919; and Marcel Duchamp, the found-sculptor and painter of *Nude Descending a Staircase*. *Others* ceased to exist in the middle of 1919. Williams himself assembled the final issue, printing Marianne Moore's "Poetry" and Stevens' "Earthy Anecdotes," plus a pair of his own red-hot editorials; but the magazine had lasted long enough, in his opinion, to put a number of struggling writers, including himself, on their feet.

During the *Others* years, Williams first began to feel his strength, to hit upon the distinctive line, the native idiom, the subject matter that would characterize his work. Leading a strenuous double life, "crowded to the full" (A, 133) with pediatrics plus three-day-a-week clinic work in the city, and in his "spare time" his writing, he nevertheless managed to produce heavily. Among the heap of verses given to *Others* were "Pastoral," the one with little sparrows hopping ingenuously about the pavement; "Touche," about the murderer's little daughter; "Old Men," those to whom he bequeathed the peaceful beer of impotence; "The Young Housewife" in her negligee calling the fish man; "El Hombre," upon which Stevens hung a poem of his own; "Danse Russe," with its cavorting of his household's happy genius; and perhaps his most memorable piece of those years—it has weathered a score of anthologies—the funeral speech, "Tract." All of these went into his third book, publication occurring once more at his own expense, *Al Que Quiere* (1917). Its title, highly tentative, meaning "to him who may want it," was brought to his mind by memories of boyhood soccer: "I was convinced nobody in the world of poetry wanted me but I was there willing to pass the ball if anyone did want it" (IWWP, 19).

Not too many stood waiting with open hands for the ball Williams passed. The "small volume" was granted notice in *Poetry*, whose review was only slightly above lukewarm, saying, "If these poems do not give the impression of titanic power or of consistent mastery, they offer certainly a fine assortment." Still, a review in *Poetry*, considering the glut of books received, was some recognition in itself, and he was found in some verses to be "marvelously observant" and "at great pains to be authentic."[11] Faint praise as it was, the hungry Williams was gratified and wrote Miss Monroe that her reviewer "really seems to have read the book and to have given it some thought."[12] The reviewer, who was Dorothy Dudley, had written of him that he appeared to have "the conscience of the great artist" but as yet lacked "the supreme ease" which ideally should accompany it. This was remarkably accurate. He was too much starved for accomplishment, for recognition, far too sensitive of his age and of the wings of time beating their staccato at his thirty-five-year-old back; and these emotions surfaced regularly in overstated essays on Art and Emotion, and in temperamental, vitriolic outbursts against critics and other practicing poets. His prose of 1919 is shrill with desperation. In "Notes from a Talk on Poetry," the poet as revolutionist is described:

> The poet goes up and down continually empty-handed. To tear down, to describe life's lies, to keep the sense bare, to attack . . . that is his job. . . . There is nothing save the emotions; I must write, I must talk when I can. It is my defiance; my love song. . . . It will not do to say, "One man is one thing, and another man is something else." That will do for life, but a poet cannot answer in that way. He is a revolutionist; he is out for truth. . . . Rhyme was a language once, but now it is a lie. It is not to be boastful that I strike out against the old, but because I must. . . . Again and again I affirm there is no importance in anything save the emotions. Play again!—I'll smash every lie you put up.[13]

In the same month that *Poetry* published the above, Williams closed the four-year life of *Others* with a final diatribe titled appropriately enough, "Belly Music," gut-reacting to everything within striking distance about him in the world of poetry. *The Lyric* is a "pink harp bespangled atrocity"; John Gould Fletcher a purveyor of "oatmeal mush"; Sandburg's work "ataxic drivel"; Mencken's poetic criticism "the braying of a superficial jackass." One suspects the trigger for his rage to have been the praise then being heaped upon another, very young, new poet, H. L. Davis of Oregon, whose "Primapara" was a current prizewinner. About the "loveliness" of a line like "the light of their dresses between quick willow leaves,"

---

[11]Dorothy Dudley, "To Whom It May Concern," *Poetry,* XII (April 1918), 39-40.
[12]Monroe, p. 389.
[13]"Notes from a Talk on Poetry," *Poetry,* XIV (July 1919), 211-16.

Williams waxed ironical, then loosed his deluge: "Oh damn loveliness. Poets have written of the big leaves and the little leaves, leaves that are red, green, yellow and the one thing they have never seen about a leaf is that it is a little engine. It is one of the things that make a plant GO" (BM, 26).

He had never taken criticism well himself. Harriet Monroe called him "the hot-blooded Mercutio of the tribe"[14] and with very good reason. When his first poems had gone to *Poetry* in 1913 and two were returned for revision, his reply was a blast, both honest and half-cocked, eight-hundred words protesting to her, "If *Poetry* does not open freely to me, in my absolute egoism, how am I to grow? . . . Anyhow, I'm a great poet, and you don't think so, and there we are."[15] But his temper was of a quick-cool variety, and soon he wrote again, complying with the request. Six years later, that chip was still perched edgily on his shoulder. Of the critics he complained: "I bunch them all as one, they are all sophomoric, puling, nonsensical. Take the best of them, Aiken, A. C. H., Hackett, Amy Lowell, what do their criticisms amount to more than an isolated perception of certain values. They pick over the dead bones" (BM, 29). And always coexisting with his temper, the nagging whisper of inadequacy persisted: that *he* was out of step, that *they* were right. "Perhaps I am a sullen suburbanite, cowardly and alone," he speculated; "I sit a blinded fool, with withered hands stretched out into the nothingness around me. Perhaps this is a sickness. Perhaps what I call my singing is a stench born out of these sores. I deny that it makes any difference. AT LEAST I AM THAT. . . . Perhaps it is all a vain regret, an insane determination to walk forward and backward at the same moment, a clinging to a youth I never enjoyed except in mad athletic excesses and stillborn ecstasies of loneliness. AT LEAST IT IS THAT" (BM, 28).

Toward The Red Wheelbarrow

Williams' introspective self-analysis, though painful, is revelatory and stunningly accurate. He was, in 1919, thirty-six years old, a married man with a growing family, a responsible pediatrician well on his way toward the 2,000 babies he would deliver during his career. Not wealthy, he was solidly successful, on the point of

---

[14] "'Others' Again," *Poetry*, XVII (December 1920), 158.
[15] *A Poet's Life*, pp. 270-71.

having "made it" professionally, able to look forward with some
ease with the better part of his struggle behind him. But it was
far from enough. He wanted more, much more, the title of his late
interviews, *I Wanted to Write a Poem*, expressing it all.

A crossroads had been reached. What did he have to show for
his travels? His third book of poems, advanced as it was over his
previous work, was scarcely the talk of the town, could not hold
a candle to the illustrious volumes that poured out since 1913
from the horde of new poets. The anthologists had not done well
by him. When Pound in 1913 sent word of his impending inclusion
in *Des Imagistes*, he wrote a friend ecstatically, "I am in it" (SL,
27); but since then, nothing but disappointment. He had appeared
in the most comprehensive collection, *The New Poetry*; seven
poems—more than some, it was true, Frost having only eight.
Stevens had three, yet two of these were already acclaimed master-
pieces. What were Williams' feeble efforts alongside "Peter Quince
at the Clavier" or "Sunday Morning"? Lindsay had five, including
the entire "Chinese Nightingale" and all of "The Congo." Amy
Lowell was represented by eleven pieces, Sandburg by eighteen,
Pound by twenty, and Masters by twenty-one. Even Adelaide
Crapsey, who had published only one slim volume, and that
posthumously, rated twelve examples of her Chinese-like invention,
the cinquain. In reviewing this anthology for *Poetry*, Williams'
friend Kreymborg took pains to praise him for his honesty, but
had to note: "As an artist, he is erratic; he has not arrived."[16] It
was disheartening enough, yet there were important collections in
which he was not considered worthy of inclusion at all. Braithwaite
was omitting him habitually from his annual volumes, and Amy
Lowell's influential *Tendencies in Modern American Poetry* (1917),
while not purporting to treat more than a select handful, contained
no mention of Williams. Two anthologies suggesting comprehensive
coverage of the new verse, Untermeyer's *Modern American Poetry*
and Jessie Rittenhouse's *Second Book of Modern Verse*, were
published in 1919. Untermeyer's collection, whose introduction
begins, " 'America's poetic renaissance' is no longer a phrase; it is
a fact," managed to gather eighty-one recent poets without including Williams, nor was there mention of him in the editorial materials. Rittenhouse's revision of her previous anthology, covering
ninety-two poets, sixty-four of them "new" since 1913, also ignored
Williams' name and poems. From Marguerite Wilkinson came the

---

[16]"As Others See Us," *Poetry*, XII (July 1919), 222.

unkindest cut of all. Her thick volume, *New Voices* (1919), included no Williams poems, but a discussion chapter, quoting four of his lines as a bad example, asked the insulting question: "Why should William Carlos Williams, who has written 'The Shadow,' 'Peace on Earth' and other tolerably good poems, be guilty of lines like the following, which, of course, are not poetry?"

In this regard 1919 was a low ebb. Yet it was also perhaps the very most apropos moment to pause and take stock, for the tide was about to turn. If Williams seemed, even to himself, a relative failure, a never-has-been, then the 1919 era marked the last time such an attitude could be held. He had broken loose from the past, his "education" was complete, his style never again was anything but his very own.

Williams' early affinity for Whitman steadily reasserted itself. A gift copy of *Leaves of Grass*, presented to the poet by his wife in 1913 and now at the University of Pennsylvania, is said to fall open naturally at "Song of Myself," whose distillation of the Whitman creed preaching individualism of person and style is the finest original example of freedom in form and vocabulary. From Whitman also, and from Hamlin Garland and the prose writers who were adventurous earlier than the modern poets, he gained the example of local American materials freely utilized without romantic shellac; this from the painters as well, whose new arrangements partook of Whitmanian self-reliance and carried it toward further boundaries. Williams' concern for structure would be at once his critical burden and his unique distinction. Whitman had set the first example, but about this time Williams noted that Sandburg was "really studying his form . . . really thinking like an artist" (SL, 41), striking for new ground rather than repeating old ways. The emphasis on radical structure which would delight his detractors throughout his career, furnishing apparently an easy mark, would also give Williams' friends pause. Even Stevens could not help remarking that he seemed "more interested in the way of saying things than in what he has to say," and he deplored the Williams who "rejects the idea that meaning has the slightest value and describes a poem as a structure of little blocks."[17] But Williams, his method by now firmly ingrained and developing fast, was not to be deterred from what he conceived to be the central issue, worthy of a poet's highest devotion and keenest wit. Structure easily became religion, "the very matter itself of a culture";

---

[17]Stevens, pp. 544, 803.

form and meaning together, inseparably interlinked, were "the very meat of a new cultural understanding" (SL, 227).

The influences shaping Williams came to a head in his acceptance of the Imagiste credo as presented in *Poetry* (1913) by Flint and Pound. So completely did their guidelines tally with his instincts, if not his previous method, that he became their principal convert. Direct treatment of the "thing" and economy of language were second nature to him; the advice to abandon "music" in favor of rhythmic structure suited to one's natural words and their meanings led ultimately to his own notion of the poetic line, at which he was a better practitioner than theorist. Pound's declaration, "The natural object is always the *adequate* symbol," is the obvious antecedent to Williams' placing so much dependence upon the red wheelbarrow and its white chickens, in pursuance of which he was at times likely to place *all* dependence upon the observed "thing" and produce poems which to Jarrell were machine parts without their machine. In so doing, Williams produced the twentieth century's most easily imitated poetry, just as the abstractionists had produced the most imitable art; in both cases, the ease was illusory, for imitation is not duplication, as a generation of would-be poets found to their chagrin. For Williams the spontaneous, objective method "worked"; others discovered that stringing snapshot prose down the page in brief snatches did not necessarily produce poetry.

After 1919 things were to look up. Depressed, but in no way persuaded to relinquish his struggle, Williams had pledged himself to art. It was, for one thing, therapeutic, a value to which his physician's training responded. "I've got to write to relieve myself of my tensions" (SL, 255), he wrote Robert McAlmon. So long as the licensed physician dealt with the precarious business of human life, orderliness was fundamental, patience a necessary virtue, and proven, established methods of procedure *de rigueur*. Beyond that, the troubled rebel that was caged during office hours had somehow to be released: "I confess I wish I could smash the hell out of where I am—but I've always felt that way and done nothing about it except write, which gives me a kind of escape." On the other hand, he had experienced no greater thrill than that of composing: "I am dead when I cannot write and when I am at it I burn with fever till one would think me mad" (SL, 256, 53). He had a chronic case.

During the twenties, Williams' fever burned steadily: *Kora in Hell, Sour Grapes, Spring and All, The Great American Novel, In the American Grain, A Voyage to Pagany* all followed rapidly, as the poet not only stepped up his production of verse but spilled over into playwriting, short stories, and the novel as well. *Others* had died, but McAlmon, recently and wealthily married, was in 1920 about to leave for France, there to publish Williams' magazine *Contact* in a first-rate format and to establish Contact Editions, which would print Williams along with other new, experimental writers. In 1922 Gorham Munson, headquartered in Vienna, began to issue *Secession*; at Matthew Josephson's suggestion, Williams out of a pile of unpublished manuscripts too radical for America furnished some of the first contributions. Josephson himself the following year, in Berlin where inflation made printing dirt-cheap, instituted his "All-American" issues of *Broom*, in which Williams' work was prominent. By the time the thirties began, he would be ready for his first *Collected Poems*.

In a way, the twenties "belonged" to Williams as the previous decade had to others. By 1920, Aiken's *Scepticisms*, a fresh survey of the new poetry by one of its prominent practitioners, began to make its impact; in the chapter "Confectionery and Caviar"— Williams included as a purveyor of the latter—Aiken praised his originality of style, even while admitting his excessive stress upon "self-expression" and the perceived object. In excluding the personal tone, to the point of depriving the reader of a poet's emotional reactions to things perceived, he seemed at times to go "floating through experience as a sensorium and nothing more." In the last analysis, however, Aiken preferred "Mr. Williams and his caviar to any amount of thin saccharine." Untermeyer fell into line in 1923; *American Poetry Since 1900* dubbed Williams an Expressionist, calling attention to his failures and somewhat erratic performance, but allowing him originality of utterance, dignity, and—despite a tendency toward exhibitionism—strength. After being ignored totally, three pages to oneself constituted progress. Never again would an anthology or a critical volume on the era be complete without him.

It was Williams' turn now, as those who had shared an earlier spotlight fell silent. Robinson concentrated on his Arthurian versions and, although he was rightly, belatedly honored, his memorable work lay behind him. Sandburg by the twenties was speaking the last of his poetic piece and turning to biography. Masters never again equalled his *Spoon River*. Amy Lowell's output declined, and, in any event, by 1925 she was dead; Lindsay ran downhill until 1931 when he took his own life gruesomely with

Lysol. Frost, the greatest self-publicist of the time, reigned, of course, but his accumulating honors rested more upon reputation than upon fresh verse. Given the normal time for recognition-lag, the field was largely Williams' and those who joined him in experimentation: Marianne Moore, E. E. Cummings, etc. Even the major poetic event of the decade, Eliot's *The Waste Land,* turned in its own way to Williams' benefit, dichotomizing poetry into two easily discernible oppositions, the spontaneous and the cerebral, by contrast revealing Williams as an indisputable leader in the former. Fond as he was of Pound, he felt that both he and Eliot by virtue of their expatriation had too impetuously escaped America for the readymade English culture that, while easing their immediate way, was in reality a trap: "They ran from something else, something cruder but, at the same time, newer, more dangerous but heavy with rewards for the sensibility that could reap them" (SL, 227).

For himself, casting his lot with America, Williams was determined—rather than follow Pound and Eliot—to portray his own land and time or nothing, like Sandburg, who seemed "to know his America and to be getting it in" (SL, 41), like Whitman in his earliest dictum. The native impulse proved right for Williams, easing the way to a body of work whose language, as Matthew Josephson has put it in *Life Among the Surrealists* (1962), "was direct, stripped of rhetoric, and had the echo of true American speech." It is this same native quality that all later commentators, whether they find Williams to their liking or too much to bear, have felt compelled to remark upon; which led Jarrell to describe him in his Introduction to *The Selected Poems,* for better or for worse, as "the America of Poets."

William Heyen

The Poet's Leap into Reality

William Carlos Williams once told Kenneth Burke about the time a group of admirers had visited him to pay him homage. It was a serious, solemn meeting; Williams' admirers were, no doubt, awed by the poet in his flesh. At parting, Williams did something that later bothered him. He gave a pretty young thing a smack on her fanny. Williams' visitors were upset, and he felt he had spoiled the occasion. But nothing could have been more in character for a poet of spontaneity who had argued against habit and convention throughout his career. The old proprieties never sufficed.

This anecdote has added dimensions. Williams was a poet of the senses, of contact—"no ideas but in things." The gesture, the affectionate smack on the girl's fanny, was a mark of the man. It should have meant only what it was. And that his own action, one that rose up from the inner man as his poems had, one perfect in itself because pure, should have bothered him was one of the contradictions residing within the poet's sensibility. Again and again he would argue, as he does in *The Descent of Winter*, that "One cannot live after a prearranged pattern, it is all dead." And so often he seems to protest too much, self-conscious about the very thin line that existed between automatic writing and his own idea of craft.

Webster Schott has edited an important book. *Imaginations* brings together five early volumes Williams published between 1920 and 1932: *Kora in Hell, Spring and All, The Great American Novel, The Descent of Winter, A Novelette and Other Prose*. All were published in small editions (*The Descent of Winter* appeared in the autumn 1928 issue of *The Exile*) and have been difficult to come by. These five experiments are, as Williams would have been the first to admit, gropings toward more mature work that would come later. But they remain significant and often rewarding in themselves. They dramatize, in addition, the problems and struggles of the artist who would later "make" (Williams' word for the creative process) such major poems as "The Desert Music," "Of Asphodel, That Greeny Flower," and, of course, the five books of *Paterson*.

From *The Saturday Review,* LIII (August 1, 1970), 21-24. Copyright 1970 Saturday Review, Inc.

Schott, in brief but balanced and informative introductions, sees the unity of Williams' work as lying in the poet's early attempts to define and exercise the imagination, without which, as Williams says again and again, we might as well number ourselves among the dead. At the same time Schott realizes that the idea of imagination unifies the five books only emotionally. In fact, wrote Williams, "Unity is the shallowest, the cheapest deception of all composition." No poet was more adamant than he in rejecting a rational theory of art, and even his statements on the imagination are usually vague. Still, *Imaginations* is as good a title as any for this book.

What does worry me a little is the editor's drift toward what I feel to be overstatement: he tells us that Williams "laid the foundation of the most consequential one-man body of modern literature in American history"; that "Without him one cannot account for contemporary American poetry." I suppose qualifiers would put me more at ease: "*one* of the most consequential bodies"; *it is difficult* to account." This is not just quibbling. Williams' early work raises the most basic questions about poetry, and from a certain point of view, if a too narrow one, it is possible to dismiss him altogether.

What we witness in *Imaginations* is the battle for pure form, for meaning indistinguishable from form, for a new poetry characterized by an imaginative leap that is itself almost beyond definition. Here is the way Williams later described it in his *Autobiography*: "The key, the master-key to the age was that jump from the feeling to the word itself: that which had been got down, the thing to be judged and valued accordingly. Everything else followed that. Without that step having been taken nothing was understandable." Nor can we move into Williams unless we realize that first and foremost he wants us to discard our preconceptions of the sources and aims of poetry.

The source of a poem, Williams argues, is its true words that well up from the poet's true self. The aim of a poem is to be itself, only itself. The point is (and I run the risk of oversimplifying here) that the poet's task is to make us see a tree, for example, in its own right—to make us see it, in other words, now and new, because habit and laziness and poor training have taken the tree away from us. So, too, with words, which have gone rotten on us, bearing the weight of muddy, traditional symbolism. ("Crude symbolism is to associate emotions with natural phenomena such as anger with lightning, flowers with love. . . . Such work is empty.") In the beginning, as Emerson said in *Nature*, each word was a poem, the perfect expression of an insight. Our words have become clichés, and the poet's only recourse is to give them back to themselves, to free them, to place them in new, more local contexts. They need new forces. They have to be freed from the conventions of logic, personal association, memory, traditional form and genre.

This, to Williams, was the essential genius of Gertrude Stein and the source of her art. "A rose is a rose is a rose." And of Juan Gris, whose grapes were grapes. It was a leap from the "sentimental" associations of language to their objective, basically denotative powers that concerned Williams. He was outraged when a committee threw Marcel Duchamp's white enamel urinal out of the Armory Show of 1913. To Williams the source of Duchamp's art was pure, its warnings deadly serious. It is a matter of our survival to see things as they are. And it is, to Williams, a matter of the highest imagination, the most sublime intelligence, to see something new, to make something new. He found no contradiction here. To see the object as it is, in its own existence, is to see it anew. And this is why "so much depends/upon" the famous red wheelbarrow and white chickens. Imaginative perception is synonymous with salvation.

The poet's repetitiousness, even shrillness, in defense of the imagination in these five books is excusable, necessary, for "Everything has a tail of difficulties that swamps the mind before expression." We come to an understanding (a bad word in regard to him, suggesting as it does logic and rationality) of Williams' major argument by a process of accretion. So much of what he says in *Imaginations* tends to illuminate the nature of the imaginative leap. He says that the symmetries of Hellenism are "too little fecundative to impregnate my world"; that he must keep his mind "free from the trammels of literature"; that T. S. Eliot's "The Love Song of J. Alfred Prufrock" and *The Waste Land* were catastrophic, setting poetry back twenty years, returning it to the stifling atmosphere of the academy; that usually there is "more sense in a sentence heard backwards than forward"; that "Fear to vary from the average, fear to feel, to see, to know, to experience— save under the opacity of a mist of equality, a mist of common mediocrity is our character." And never must we think that the imaginative leap is a flight from reality. Just the opposite is true. The modern artist has to strike to the bone of the thing itself, to its essential "thingness."

Even though, in *The Great American Novel*, Williams condemned the "complacent Concordites" for being too imitative, I become more and more convinced that the roots of his art, both technical and thematic, are to be found in Emerson and Thoreau. For one thing, Emerson realized that his was Talent (the ability to make meters and rhymes) rather than true Genius (the flame of poetic inspiration), and the whole brunt of Emerson's aesthetic as set forth in "The Poet," an essay that remains central to our time, puts Williams within basic Emersonian tradition. Poetry, said Emerson, stems from "a thought so passionate and alive that like the spirit of a plant or animal it has an architecture of its own, and adorns nature with a new thing." This is not, I take it, a statement of Aristotelian imitation. Williams himself, in *Spring and All* and again in his *Autobiography*, attacks Hamlet's view that art must "hold a mirror up to nature." Art, says Williams, must make a new thing.

Two other points. First, we remember that it was Emerson who greeted Whitman at the beginning of his great career. The vulgar Walt, who could write lines like "Fog in the air, beetles rolling balls of dung" and "The scent of these armpits aroma finer than prayer," and who could celebrate the miracle of digestion and the "Firm masculine colter," exploded the boundaries of poetry's subject matter once and for all. Emerson was glad to see him do it. This breaking of boundaries led Williams to lines that merged what was traditionally considered beautiful and proper with what was considered ugly and squalid: "the moon is in/the oak tree's crotch." Williams' formulation of beauty as being the inner perfection of a thing, his perception that "syphilis is no more than a wild pink in the rock's cleft," his realization, finally, that to make poetry and to render beauty one had to point to the "inimitable particles of dissimilarity to all other things which are the peculiar perfections of the thing in question," as he says in *Kora in Hell*, stem from Emerson as aesthetician and Whitman as practitioner.

Also, Williams is an "organic" poet, as these five books attest. He sings the praises of inspiration and has faith that the form one of his works finally achieves, if he has the genius to allow his words to free themselves, to dance, will be the right and only form. It is Emerson, and later the Whitman of "Song of Myself," who clear the way for Williams' proem improvisations in *Kora in Hell*, his interweaving of prose and poetry in *Spring and All* and *The Descent of Winter*, his great American fractured prose non-novel *The Great American Novel*, his automatic writing in *A Novelette*.

If Williams does, indeed, adorn nature with new things, the American Transcendentalists justify his meter, subjects, forms, intentions. He cried out for an American poetry of words firmly wedded to a place, a locale, and said that the Concordites were too European. It may very well be that their European roots were not as deep as his own.

Williams had already spent a year and a half in Switzerland and France by the time he entered the University of Pennsylvania in 1902. There he met Ezra Pound and Hilda Doolittle, studied and copied Keats religiously, and began to realize that medicine would be the proper career to complement his life as a poet. The choice wasn't an easy one. Many of his contemporaries believed that the road to freedom led to Bohemia. But in *Spring and All* Williams writes: "The better work men do is always done under stress and at great personal cost." Doc Williams was a physician of great dedication, but always, between patients or late at night, he wrote, and prolifically. His life as a doctor brought him close to the common, close to essentials, and words flooded him. The act of writing was itself meaning and affirmation and even personal therapy. The more trying the time, the more demanding was the poet's urge to release the words. When making house calls he carried a yellow notebook with him to capture the images that inundated him.

He lamented the fact that the new could not get a hearing, that established critics ignored modernism or missed the point. Even Pound, though he somewhat admired what he called Williams' "opacity," asked Williams how a reader of good intentions could come to grips with the improvisations of *Kora in Hell*. To be sure, in *Imaginations* the poet often seems extremely self-conscious about not making in his own work the usual kinds of sense demanded of art. But he went on, throwing in his lot with the avant-garde journals, distrusting the intellect, detesting closed or imposed forms. He was convinced that poetry must, and could, reach out for an objective method. Damn the critics and the stagnant American cultural scene! Full speed ahead! He was confident that work of real value would win out. It had to.

Life, for Williams, would not stand still enough to be true to systems of logic. The poetry of thought was artificial and, therefore, dead. Though Yvor Winters would come, in 1965, to dismiss him as an "anti-intellectual," someone who "did not know what intellect was," Williams' intuition had early brought him toward a concept of the place of idea in poetry from which he could not

waver. He saw Marianne Moore as most consistently the consum-
mate American artist. She, "wiping soiled words or cutting them
clean out, removing the aureoles that have been pasted about
them or taking them bodily from greasy contexts," made a poetry
of the highest intelligence. She is concerned, writes Williams, with
"the hard and unaffected concept of the apple itself as an idea. . . ."
This is Williams' praise of a poet who knew enough to make the
imaginative leap to a higher level of truth. Miss Moore, he argues,
"launched her thought not to have it appear arsenaled as in a text-
book on psychology, but to stay among apples and giraffes in a
poem." It is a mark of our mediocrity if we are uncomfortable
when we cannot isolate the didactic qualities of a poem.

These five books take away from us even the comfort of being
able to come to grips with them generically. Williams revised
slightly or not at all, fearing that the ogre of sense would rise up
from the page. *Kora in Hell* consists of improvisations—anything
that came to Williams each night over a year—, many followed by
what he called "interpretations." But the interpretations are
themselves almost entirely free from explanation. The poet is
highly inventive, his words gush out and leap. But the method
frequently wears thin. At such times Williams reminds me of the
Mr. Imagination of that children's television show of years ago,
who loaded up his train with kiddies for the trip to various never-
never lands. Williams seems to be saying something, arguing something, and then floods the ground under our feet.

Spring and All has much the same effect. There are brilliant,
dazzling passages of prose, and there are poems that many of us
know and have come to admire: "By the road to the contagious
hospital," "The rose is obsolete," and the poem that begins "The
pure products of America/go crazy—" and ends

> Somehow
> it seems to destroy us
>
> It is only in isolate flecks that
> something
> is given off
>
> No one
> to witness
> and adjust, no one to drive the car

It is true that Williams began *Spring and All* as a parody of various
styles of the time, but chapters out of order, a Roman numeral

placed upside down, the constant and purposeful descent into unintelligibility, the catalogues of insignificant images—these things often prove too trying, and the book as a whole remains a pastiche. When I say this, of course, Williams is ready to make me feel foolish. His aesthetic presupposes that I need to make the proper imaginative leap, and I have to realize that, as he says in *Kora in Hell*, "The virtue of it all is in an opening of the doors, though some rooms of course will be empty. . . ."

The Great American Novel has no plot and seems to go nowhere. It is a hodgepodge of an antinovel, and reads as though the poet had made a list of novelistic conventions in order to avoid them. Here and there we glimpse a decadent America, the poet clutching at words to maintain his sanity. But the book has no major concern, no center of gravity except to be itself a manifestation of the new. This is as Williams intended it, of course. "si la sol fa mi re do. . . . Substitution of something else. What? Well, nonsense. Since you drive me to it." *The Great American Novel* is an answer to system, a disruption of habitual perception. It speaks for itself and for Williams' beliefs and intentions when it says: "It is at least the beginning of art." Nothing of value, Williams declares, can be created before our termite-ridden structures are destroyed.

A Novelette and Other Prose goes, it seems to me, just as far (a long journey or a short one, depending on how you take your choice after you pay your money), but no further. One thing, in the end, is certain: if we should praise a poet for achieving his intentions, Williams deserves high praise indeed. The critical rub occurs, of course, when we begin questioning these intentions. For some of us the traditional notion of unity remains a virtue, and poetry is still a communication on a rational as well as irrational level.

Some of the finest prose and poetry in *Imaginations* is in the form of journal entries in *The Descent of Winter*, which Williams began while on board ship in the fall of 1927, returning from Europe, where he'd left his family. The poet, entering middle age, again feels the need to get something down, anything. He's depressed, worried about the particular kind of work he wants to do and the possibility of an audience. He wants "to do work so excellent that by its excellence it repels all idiots but idiots are like leaves and excellence of any sort is a tree when the leaves fall the tree is naked and the wind thrashes it until it howls it cannot get a book published it can only get poems into certain magazines that are suppressed. . . ."

Williams exercises his imagination by pointing out the profound relationship that exists between an industrialized society in which "the office-workers in cotton running pants get in a hot car, ride in a hot tunnel and confine themselves in a hot office—to sell asphalt," and the sorry state of the society's poetry. For our actions have become automatic, machinelike, habitual, and poetry has become "a soft second light of dreaming." Williams continues to define the ills of our age and in so doing to define and further refine his aesthetic. "The sagas," he says, "seem to have been made on the spot." They do not stultify us with the feeling that we are being smothered with technique, as the workers' jobs do. It is imperative that we escape the superficial and descend to true meaning again. Williams yearns for "simple clarity of expression." The problem is that "To be plain is to be subverted since every term must be forged new, every word is tricked out of meaning, hanging with as many cheap traps as an altar." In life and in art the problems are the same and have the same causes. Dr. Williams felt that words needed a physician as badly as did the sick.

One of the most marvelous sections in *The Descent of Winter* describes the world into which one Dolores Marie Pischak is born in Fairfield. The child is brought into a scene as spontaneous and hectic as the best poems, says Williams, "among insults, brawls, yelling, kicks, brutality—here the old dignity of life holds on— defying the law, defying monotony." And this is life, this is love, this is the disorderly order of things and the inspiration for a new poetry. Here, where Dolores Marie was born, people are still alive but need only look out their windows to see the spreading death: "order triumphant, one house like another, grass cut to pay love-lessly." By finding out what he has to say through writing, Williams in this volume sees as clearly as he ever does his own need to pursue those values he knows and feels are right.

What is it that we demand from our poets? This, I suppose, is the primary question these five early Williams volumes pose for us. The poet is insistent, telling us that the world does not have room for both "conventional" and "new" poets. The former can lead us only to death, hell, and winter; the latter point the way to life, heaven, spring. The imagination, he argues, is our means to a dynamic existence. What is necessary is cleavage—from the past, from the mind and its rote drudgery, and images of cleavage abound in the poems and prose of *Imaginations*. Williams here has written primarily to destroy, feeling that life and art have become not only superficial and meaningless, but cancerous, deadly.

The reader of *Imaginations* is likely himself to come away with mixed feelings. Much here is unquestionably brilliant, but often the patients, the volumes themselves as manifestations of all that they argue, seem to die of such radical cures.

Charles Angoff

A Williams Memoir

Years ago, when I was an editor of the *American Mercury*, Dr. William Carlos Williams sent in a half dozen poems. Three of us read them. We all thought they were not his best work. We were all very sorry. We all had high respect for him, and we all wanted to get him into the pages of the *Mercury*. We all thought we would be doing him an injustice by printing the poems he sent us. I was especially sorry about the fix we were in, for I had for a long time been drawn to his work. I offered to write to him as diplomatic a letter as possible. I wrote that letter. I tried to make it especially clear that we wanted very much to have him in the pages of the *Mercury*. Almost by return mail I got a postcard reply from Dr. Williams. Unfortunately, I lost the card. But I do remember the general content of the card. He called me "a damn fool," and he called the *Mercury* "a stupid magazine to which no decent person would care to contribute." I replied that we still wanted very much to have him in the magazine, and asked him to send us more poems and any prose he wanted to have published. I told him that I liked his book of sketches and stories, *In the American Grain*, very much. He never replied.

Some months later Weldon Kees, a poet of considerable power, called me on the telephone. He had lived in Colorado, I believe, and now was living in New York City. He wanted to see me. We met. He reminded me of some letters I had written him several years before. He had just begun to write poetry and was

Reprinted by permission from *Prairie Schooner*, XXXVIII (Winter 1964-65), 299-305. Copyright © 1965 by the University of Nebraska Press.

pleased by my polite handling of his poems. I hadn't accepted
them, but I had shown an interest. He had been encouraged.
He wanted to say thank you. I was pleased. Then he asked me
if I knew Dr. William Carlos Williams. I told him about the
above episode. Nevertheless, I offered to write a letter to Dr.
Williams, introducing Weldon Kees. I asked Kees whether he
wanted to take this chance. He said, "Sure." To my great surprise
I got a very friendly card from Dr. Williams. Yes, he would be
glad "to see anybody whom you like. As they say, a friend of yours
is a friend of mine." I didn't quite know how to take this note.
I decided to take it at face value.

Weldon Kees saw Dr. Williams. He told me about the meeting.
"Say," said Kees, "he's a very good friend of yours. I thought
you two had never met."

"We never had," I said.

"That's funny," said Kees. "He spoke as if you two had known
each other for years."

"No, I had never met him," I insisted. "Did he say anything
about that unpleasant . . . ."

"Oh, yes, sort of. He said you two had had some words. He
was sorry that he had made a fool of himself."

When the *Literary Review*, of which Dr. Clarence R. Decker
and I are co-editors, was founded, I approached Dr. Williams for
a contribution or two to the first issue. I thought I would have
some trouble. So I began by pointing out to him that Fairleigh
Dickinson University, sponsor of the magazine, was situated in
Rutherford, New Jersey (that is, the mother campus was), that
he was a Rutherfordian, and we wanted to do him honor by
featuring him in the first issue.

"Why, sure, Charlie," he said, smiling somewhat shyly. "You
don't have to give me that spiel. Sure, I'll be glad to appear
in the first issue. Hell, you don't have to give me all that spiel.
Hell, no.

I thought he blushed as he said all this. I had the feeling that
his innermost being, for some vague reason, was not too happy
with his blustering good fellowship. It was the first time that
I met him. I had called him on the telephone, and he asked me
to come over. His wife met me at the door, and she, too, was most
friendly. I had the feeling that Flossie, his wife, was the business
person at 9 Ridge Road, that she sort of ran him. Compared to
her husband she was firm. Dr. Williams appeared to be shy.
Almost pleadingly he said to his wife, "Won't you give Charlie

a drink?" Then he turned to me and said, "I like bourbon, do you? As a matter of fact, all the whiskeys are pretty good." I asked for a bourbon highball.

He let me have virtually anything he had available on hand. One of the truly fine things he gave us was a sketch of his mother. It is one of his most memorable prose pieces.

I suggested to Dr. Sammartino that he give Dr. Williams an honorary degree. I did this through Dr. Decker, the vice-president. Dr. Williams was enormously pleased. Somewhat later I saw him and said how nice it was for him to accept the honorary degree and I said the obvious thing, "By accepting it you did the University honor."

"Hell, no," he said, "they honored me. I was just thrilled to get it. Hell, I'm a Rutherfordian, don't you ever forget it." He smiled. "I was wondering how much longer I would have to wait. You know I'm not a well man."

I learned later how unwell he was. He had had a severe heart attack some years before. Now and then, I was told, he had little strokes that laid him low for a while, but fortunately, he eventually got out of them, without any outward permanent damage. Somebody told me that one day he would have one stroke too many and that would be the end. I asked my informant if Dr. Williams knew that. "Sure he does. He told me about it."

I was associated with the Writer's Conference at Wagner College, on Staten Island, in New York City for four years. The third year it occurred to me that it would be a good idea if Dr. Williams would come over to address the students. For some strange reason I forgot, for the moment, that he was an unwell man, and called his house. His wife answered. I told her why I called. "Oh," she said, "but Bill is sick. He's been in bed for the past couple of days. I mean . . . ." She stopped, and I overheard her talking to somebody, though I couldn't hear the exact words passed. The next voice I heard was that of Dr. Williams. "Hello," he said.

I was embarrassed. I said, "I'm sorry. I didn't know. I mean . . . ."

"Don't apologize, Charlie," he said. "A little sickness between friends is nothing. What was it you wanted?"

I told him, and again apologized.

"Never mind the apologizing," he said. "I'll be glad to come over. Only there are two conditions." I heard him laugh. "Only two conditions," he repeated. "Are you sitting down?"

"Yes, why?"

"Well, the first condition is that you have a chauffeur pick me up and bring me back."

"That's easy," I said. "Granted. Now what's the second condition?"

"Are you sitting down?"

"Yes."

"Really sitting down?"

"Yes. Why?"

"Good, the second condition is that you get me a bottle of Wilson's whiskey. It doesn't have to be Wilson's, but I just happened to think of it. It's as good as any."

I hesitated. Wagner College is a Lutheran-sponsored college, and I had heard some stories about some of its preacher trustees. They had the reputation of being "strict." The rule apparently was that drinking was absolutely forbidden on campus, but that professors could "indulge" outside the campus, "with moderation, of course." The catch was that the conference was housed at a girls' dormitory on campus, and obviously getting a bottle of whiskey on campus and in a girls' dormitory was "out of order."

"Well?" asked Dr. Williams.

"I don't know," I said. "That really is a problem. You see, we are staying at a dormitory, and drinking is forbidden, and . . . I just don't know what to say."

He laughed. Then he said, "Those are my conditions."

I hesitated, then I said, "All right. I promise I'll get you the bottle of whiskey. It's entirely illegal, and I don't know how I'll manage it. I just don't really know. But I'll get it for you."

"Good boy," said Dr. Williams. "Good boy."

I solved my problem by merely telling Gorham Munson what I planned to do. Gorham smiled. "Oh, get the whiskey. It's, let us say, illegally legal. Nothing will happen."

I got the whiskey. I got a room for Dr. Williams in the girls' dormitory. He asked me to fill a half tumbler with straight whiskey—no "adulterants" such as water or soda or ginger ale. He took it down almost in one gulp. I marveled at him. His face became flushed and for a few moments I was worried. Then he said, "Now, let me get at your students."

He was magnificent in his talk before the students. He spoke to them in the open on a portico facing New York harbor. He was on his feet for almost an hour and a half. His voice was strong. He spoke cogently, poetically, brilliantly. He discussed the essence of poetry. He gave examples of good poetry and of bad poetry. He answered questions—quickly, politely, but incisively. He received a long and obviously sincere ovation.

I invited him to dinner after his talk. "I hope you're hungry," I said. "I am, but a little drink would help me along," he said.

I managed to sneak down a good stiff drink for him, and I saw at once that alcohol was exactly what he needed. He ate a fine dinner and his conversation was lively.

I put him back in the automobile about nine o'clock. I apologized for the late hour. "Not at all," he said. "I loved it."

Without his knowing I had brought down the remainder of the bottle of whiskey, and as he made himself comfortable in the automobile I gave him what was left of the bottle.

"You're a sweetheart, Charlie," he said. "Just a sweetheart. I was wondering what was going to happen to the bottle. I think I'll take another drink before I go off to bed."

Not long later I had a poem in the *Arizona Quarterly*. It was entitled "Silence." Shortly after it was published I got a letter from Dr. Williams telling me how much he had liked it. Professor Margaret Coit, a colleague on the faculty of Fairleigh Dickinson University, a few days later told me that he had talked about the poem at length one night when several people were visiting the Williamses. I wrote Dr. Williams a note thanking him for his note. He wrote back and said he had long been an admirer of my work, and he added, "After all, you and I are the most frequent contributors to little magazines in the country. We must stick together."

News reached the East that Weldon Kees had committed suicide. I had not heard from him for a long time. He had left New York City for the Pacific Coast and had sent me only occasional cards or brief notes. Once he had asked me to send him whatever writings I came across that had to do with suicide. I did send him some pieces. I put no especial importance to his request. I was only helping out a friend.

When the news of his suicide reached me this request of his came back to my mind—and now it made a grisly sort of sense.

A few days later I was at Dr. Williams' home, and I brought up the matter of Kees's suicide. "It puzzles me," I said. "It puzzles me and it pains me, you know what I mean."

Dr. Williams looked at me, his eyes became bright, he turned his head, then he faced me and said, "I don't understand it, I really don't. All he had to do is kiss his wife or wait for the sunset."

I went to Dr. Williams' funeral. I was heartsick. Chiefly because his own wishes about funerals had not been followed. In a poem called "Tract" he had suggested that no flowers be placed on a man's coffin, but something he really cared for, old clothes, or a book, or something else he cherished.

Dr. Williams' own coffin was covered with flowers. There were no old clothes, no book. But then it occurred to me that he would not have been angry. He was a man of outbursts, some of them violent—as when he denounced Robert Frost as "an old fogey"— but if one waited a few moments he would take back what he had said. He was a true democrat. He loved Rutherford and he loved people and he loved small towns and he loved America and he was disturbed by God's mysterious plans—but whenever serious doubts assailed him he kissed his wife and he waited for the sunset—and he was happy again.

Eric Mottram

The Making of *Paterson*

The letters of William Carlos Williams from 1936 onwards show again and again his difficulty in embarking on and completing "that magnum opus I've always wanted to do: the poem *Paterson*." In 1936 he tells Ezra Pound "I've been sounding myself out in these years working toward a form of some sort," and it was the form rather than the materials, the kind of line, rhythm and overall structure rather than the series of dramatized themes, which worried him. Aware of the contemporary large-scale, inclusive works by Stevens, Eliot, Pound and others, he had to consider the nature of the "order" his poem would take. It would be unlike Stevens' "Parts of a World," he writes in 1943, "a looser, wider world, where 'order' is a servant not a master. Order is what is discovered after the fact, not a little piss pot for us all to urinate into and call ourselves satisfied." But by 1947, after the publication of *Paterson* Book One in 1946, he can write that "the whole

From *Stand*, Quarterly 7, Number 3 (1965), pp. 17-34. Reprinted by permission of the journal.

of the form of the four books has been roughly sketched out for several years," and he is more confident about the style of his form (in a letter to Kenneth Burke) emerging from "a desire . . . to find some basis for avoiding the tyranny of the symbolic without sacrificing fullness of imagery." His safeguard against this tyranny was to be unsymbolized facts, facts as instances in the manner his "objectivist" poetic practice and theory had been presenting since *Spring and All* in 1923.

As late as 1960, speaking of Villon's poetry and speaking for Villon as well as himself, it seems now, Williams is still stressing the place of fact in poems: "the facts are there, properly named if a man has the courage to use them with art enough; and I have the courage and the art—and time to use it." But of course it is just there that Williams differed from Villon: time is what the town doctor did not have. Yet he did not want to be a full-time artist working on his "magnum opus": "I have defeated myself purposely in almost everything I do," he says to John Thirlwall, "because I didn't want to be thought an *artist*. I much prefer to be an ordinary person. I never wanted to be separated from my fellow mortals by acting like an artist. I never wanted to be an artist externally—only secretly so as not to be set apart. I wanted to be something rare but not to have it separate me from the crowd." In this way his facts would be experienced items of living, of "felt life," from the life of a city doctor who could say with Whitman "I am the man, I suffered, I was there," and not the pre-ordered facts of his friend's *Cantos* or Eliot's aristocratic religious order.

"He was a curiously factual person": Williams' remark about Villon holds for him too. He hoped facts and named life objects would enable his large poem to keep a hold on truths to life, especially since he belonged to no dogmatic doctrine of religion, philosophy or economic-political theory. His only security was his daily factual life and the facts of certain forms of art: Whitman's linear examples, the French dislocutions and reassemblages of facts in Surrealist poetry, and Cubist painting. "In literature," he wrote, "there can be no seeking for words. For a writer to so indulge himself is to tread dangerous ground."

Williams was not an isolated man as a Rutherford doctor: he knew well at some time or other in his life the writers Pound, Marianne Moore, Gertrude Stein, Ford Madox Ford, Joyce, Cummings, Djuna Barnes and Mina Loy, all but the last three engaged at some point in their lives in a large-scale inclusive work; but he also knew well the painters Charles Demuth, Marsden Hartley,

Charles Sheeler, Gleizes and Marcel Duchamp. He also admired
Villon, Chaucer, and Whitman as "contemporaries of mind with
whom I am constantly in touch—through the art of writing." As
far back as 1930 Williams writes of the poet's vocation with all the
seriousness with which the medical profession is taken in his 1928
novel *A Voyage to Pagany*. While speaking of Jung he says that in
the year of the Depression, in the middle of international catastrophe already impending disaster, the air full of Spenglerian inti-
mations of Western decline, he affirms that

> it is he, the poet, whose function it is, when the race has gone
> astray, to lead it—to destruction perhaps, but in any case, to
> lead it.
>   This he will not do by mere blather but by a magnificent
> organization of those materials his age has placed before him for
> his employment.
>   At the same time he usually invents a technique. Or he seems
> to do so. But really it is that he has been the fortunate one who
> has gathered all the threads together that have been spun for
> many centuries before him and woven them into his design . . .
>   On the poet devolves the most vital function of society: to
> recreate it—the collective world—in time of stress, in a new mode,
> fresh in every part, and so set the world working or dancing or
> murdering each other again, as it may be.

Here, in "Caviar and Bread Again: A Warning to the New
Writer," the forty-seven year old poet is moving towards his
master work with the right ambition, but Pound is there before
him, and in 1931 it is clear that he relates the *Cantos* to his own
ambition when he describes their action and makes an implied
criticism of Eliot's poetic position:

> Pound has had the discernment to descry and the mind to grasp
> that the difficulties in which humanity finds itself need no phenom-
> enal insight for their solution. Their cure is another matter, but
> that is no reason for a belief in a complicated mystery of approach
> fostered by those who wish nothing done, as it is no reason for
> a failure of the mind to function simply when dangerously
> confronted. Here is a theme: a closed mind which clings to its
> power—about which the intelligence beats seeking entrance. This
> is the basic theme of the *XXX Cantos*. (*Excerpts from a
> Critical Sketch.*)

Pound's purposes are projected in his own "measure" and "movement," themselves part of the inevitable meaning in the poetry, Williams goes on to say, noticing how Pound solves problems of continuity between levels and kinds of material in a single large construction:

> He can include pieces of prose and have them still part of a *poem*. It is incorporated in a movement of the intelligence which is special, beyond usual thought and action—
> It partakes of a quality which makes the meter, the movement peculiar—unmeasurable (without a prior change of mind)—
> It is that which is the evidence of invention. Pound's line is the movement of his thought, his concept of the whole.

The *Cantos* are like *Paterson* is to be, traditionally "serious" in that here you have "a solution in some sense of the continuous confusion and barrenness which life imposes in its mutations—(on him who will not create)." The generation of the poet's solution is "analytical," not simply "mass fusion" or even "synthesis" at any profound level: this is Pound's "chief distinction in the *Cantos* —his personal point of departure from most that the modern is attempting. It is not by any means a synthesis, but a shot through all material—a true and somewhat old-fashioned analysis of his world."

But Pound's use of past examples of good government and clarity of behavior was not Williams' way: "You build houses, for people. Poems are the same" (*The Basis of Faith in Art*, 1937). He needed to find a form which presented people, in action in the present, but in a city built on a site with a local history and geography from which universals could be made without imposing on them an ideology drawn from dogma or some synthesis from doctrines. "By his structure he shows this struggle," the struggle to find a form of measure and compositional continuity: Williams is here writing about Dante's great structure (*Against the Weather*, 1939) and he adds:

> the artist's is the great master pattern which all others approach and in this Dante and the archpriest are the same. The moral good and bad approach the good and bad of the arts. Formal patterns of all sorts represent arrests of the truth in some particular phase of its mutations, and immediately thereafter, unless they change, become mutilations.

Therefore the facts have to be shown in continuous change: the structure must not be a closed plot, either cyclic or ending in catastrophe or prophetic of disastrous conclusion. As Williams put it, "this is the principal objective of a work of art—to maintain this [the great pattern] against the weather of the other conditions—so that though they warp and bend it the effect will be still the supersedure of that above these effects . . . Man has only one enemy: the weather."

Working on the early books of *Paterson* it became clear that the structure being created combined two personal innovations: a conception of measure and a conception of poetic continuity which would be competent to handle both the social and the personal life of the poem. In "The Poem as a Field of Action" (1948), Williams speaks of his need "to seek (what we believe is there) a new measure or a new way of measuring that will be commensurate with the social, economic world in which we are living as contrasted with the past." The measure is both line and volume delineating the facts and retaining their life. Williams later criticized Carl Sandburg's *Collected Poems*—and Sandburg had attempted a human epic structure in *The People, Yes*—as "formless as a drift of desert sand engulfing the occasional shrub or tree . . . a dunelike mass . . . his characters, a drift of people, a nameless people for the most part, are sand, giving the wind form in themselves until they lie piled up filling his pages." Perhaps he was also remembering Robert Lowell's criticism of *Paterson* Book One in a letter of 1947: "it is a defect perhaps that human beings exist almost entirely in the prose passages." As Williams acknowledged, "that's something to think about."

Besides this decade or more of essays preparing for *Paterson,* Williams carried on a continual correspondence about his work, until 1956 and perhaps beyond, with a number of American critics and poets, including Parker Tyler, Babette Deutsch, Horace Gregory, Jose Garcia Villa, Sister Bernetta Quinn, John C. Thirlwall and Robert Lowell. Although the general scaffolding of *Paterson* had been worked out, Williams retained his empirical methods and attitudes as the work went forward like a moving core in his life as a doctor, husband, father, literary man and correspondent of friends. It is a deeply social poem; its characters are part of the New Jersey town and part of the unstable thirties and forties. The general ideas which thread through the five books are human notions—for example, the definition of deformity, the metaphor of divorce, the flow of the river from mountain source through its falls and the polluting city to the undifferentiating sea, the man Paterson as protagonist of the city Paterson, and the natural site of the city, all as ways of finding "some basis for avoiding the tyranny of the symbolic without sacrificing fulness of imagery."

The city is the instance of a man and the imaginative conception of a man's lifetime in history and geography. It is distinctly unlike Eliot's fearful resentment of a city and more like Mumford's less agrarian, less Christian, but still wary, appreciation of the city as the major instance of what men have been able to achieve. Paterson is "a man of some intelligence," not an abstraction or a convenient peasant or urban sloven of romantic primitivism which hopes to reduce a man to his abstraction "man."

In 1926 Williams wrote a short poem called *Paterson* which appeared in *The Dial,* and although he did deny later that this was an origin of the later work, it does contain the basic city-river difference and the fundamental, repeated idea "Say it, no ideas but in things," the whole theory and practice of *Paterson.* (There is a conflict here between his statement to Edith Heal in *I Wanted to Write a Poem* (1958) and his *Autobiography* (1951) in which he refers to the earlier *Paterson* "on which I based the later and more extended poem.") The last lines of the 1926 poem read something like a basis for the later work:

> What wind and sun of children stamping the snow
> stamping the snow and screaming drunkenly
> The actual, florid detail of cheap carpet
> amazingly upon the floor and paid for
> as no portrait ever was—Canary singing
> and geraniums in tin cans spreading their leaves
> reflecting red upon the frost—
> They are the divisions and imbalances
> of his whole concept, made small by pity
> and desire, they are—no ideas beside the facts—

These last three lines are the theme which is given in the opening italicized section preceding *Paterson* Book One and which, in fact, are there too in the general scheme for the whole work, comprising a sense of locality, the four seasons chronology, the river's course to the sea, "a confession; a basket; a column," and a linguistic artistic idea—"a reply to Greek and Latin with the bare hands." The whole celebration is to be "in distinct terms; by multiplication, a reduction to one." This scheme, like the poem, is "a plan for action to supplant a plan for action; a taking up of slack; a dispersal and a metamorphosis." The gist is that the poetic action should be its own plot. The field of action and the measure allow the characters and ideas to live without compunction, controlled only by the poet's compassion or repugnance, as he guides himself through "the weather." As he remarked to Edith Heal, "the idea was a metaphysical conception; how to get that into a form probably came gradually."

Paterson became one of those persistent efforts of major American poets to create the epic poem of their personal vision: Hart Crane's *The Bridge* (written partly in response to *The Waste Land*), Stevens' *Notes Towards a Supreme Fiction* with its complementary poems *Esthétique du Mal, Credences of Summer* and *The Man with the Blue Guitar*, Sandburg's *The People, Yes*, Frost's *New Hampshire* and *Build Soil* (and perhaps the two equivocal *Masques*), and more recently Muriel Rukeyser's *Waterlily Fire* and Buckminster Fuller's *Untitled Epic Poem on the History of Industrialization*. In the last decade we can add Charles Olson's *Maximus* sequence, Robert Nichol's *Slow Newsreel of a Man Riding a Train* and, above all, Allen Ginsberg's *Howl, Kaddish* and *Siesta in Xbalba* sequence. The "blessed rage for order" continues to exert its power in American poets in search of a meaningful vision during a time of catastrophe and enforced ideology. Each of these poems and sequences has its ordering problem. Crane seeks a vision of a technological new world of light within which the great American myths and mythological men and women can be living instances of creative energy against the forces of destruction. Pound constructs a huge journal in the form of a periplum, coasting varieties of civilized experience and poised momentarily in lyrical cadences of relief in traditional beauty. Stevens, nearer to Williams, creates a language out of groups of possible definitions of an entirely flexible, humanist ideal of a "major man," without dogma, continually exploring, using art as Eliot's *Four Quartets* suggests a man should use the *Via Media* mystical tradition. Stevens uses the physical nature of localities to anchor his vision, but *Paterson* is nearer the use of Dublin in *Ulysses*, as a map of a metaphysical idea of remembered actual life, backed by reading. *Paterson* has a significant colonial history, a river with its falls, a line of Indian and white American figures and their tales, and a published history (through the Historical Society of Paterson). The pattern is there in the city ready to be used. But although each part of the poem was planned as a unit complete in itself, reporting the progress of the river, Williams told Edith Heal that "finally, I let the form take care of itself; the colloquial language, my own language, set the pace."

At the outset of his career Williams had discarded a long Keatsian narrative poem and preferred to begin his collected works with his first long poem, which led to *Paterson*, "The Wanderer," which contains already the Passaic river and other features of what Conrad Aiken calls the "ur-Paterson." It hardly projects a personal language yet, and the ideas seem to have been molded through Whitman's New York poems. The rhetoric is very literary. Even the 1913 strike of the Paterson silk-workers is treated obliquely. The clearest factual line is simply "The Passaic, that filthy river," which the wanderer-poet enters and traces from "crystal beginning" to its "degradation" and which becomes the draught of knowledge, including the knowledge of his own death. In a 1947 letter to Babette Deutsch, Williams refers her to "The Strike" and the prose "Life along the Passaic River" for more details of "the social unrest" which is strong in *Paterson*, especially in Book One part three. He is quite explicit about this factor and its treatment in the poem:

> . . . much more relating to the economic distress occasioned by human greed and blindness—aided, as always, by the church, all churches in the broadest sense of that designation—but still, there will be little treating directly of the rise of labor as a named force. I am not a Marxian.

He describes his general handling of social material in a letter to Robert McAlmon in 1943: "an account, a psychologic-social panorama of a city treated as if it were a man, the man Paterson."

But his letters from 1936 onwards complain frequently of the frustrations in getting the poem written at all, of "gradually maneuvering a mass of material . . . to the impossible poem *Paterson*" (to Wallace Stevens in 1944). It was mainly the lack of time at his disposal and the exhaustion he knew would follow his beginning to compose, rather than arrange, his material. The longer he left it the more he found he himself had changed: "the old approach is outdated," he writes to Horace Gregory in 1945, "and I shall have to work like a fiend to make myself new again. But there is no escape. Either I remake myself or I am done. I

can't escape the dilemma longer. THAT is what has stopped me.
I must go on or quit once and for all."

The obsession ran deep and it concerned his need to see the
pattern in his necessarily day-to-day contingent life: a busy professional man at work in two fields of action—medicine and
poetry—two ways of grasping and changing reality:

> for the poet there are no ideas but in things . . . the poet does
> not . . . permit himself to go beyond the thought to be discovered
> in the context of that with which he is dealing: no ideas but in
> things. The poet thinks with his poem, in that lies his thought. . . .
> The thought is *Paterson,* to be discovered there.

This passage from the *Autobiography* (1951) exactly repeats
his appreciation of Pound in 1931 and the chapter is in fact called
The Poem Paterson and describes how its genesis appeared to him
later:

> The first idea centering upon the poem, *Paterson,* came alive early:
> to find an image large enough to embody the whole knowable
> world about me. The longer I lived in my place, among the details
> of my life, I realized that these isolated observations and experi-
> ences needing pulling together to gain "profundity."

Manhattan or New York was "far out of my perspective" and
Rutherford too near. But on the familiar river lay Paterson:

> I wanted, if I was to write in a larger way than of the birds and
> flowers, to write about the people close about me: to know in
> detail, minutely what I was talking about—to the whites of their
> eyes, to their very smells.
>
> That is the poet's business. Not to talk in vague categories but
> to write particularly, as a physician works, upon a patient, upon
> the thing before him, in the particular to discover the universal.

In 1945 he had written to Norman Macleod that "Dewey might
do something for me," and now he places himself firmly in that
American philosopher's tradition of pragmatic instrumentalism:
"John Dewey had said (I discovered it quite by chance), 'The
local is the only universal, upon that all art builds'." Paterson was
local, with living colonial history upstream where the Passaic was
clean, and downstream the products of Hamilton's fiscal and indus-

trial policies. In the park, Williams remembered hearing Billy Sunday and talking to John Reed. As a gynecologist he had worked in local hospitals and as a young man he walked and swam on Garret Mountain. He had even appeared in court in Paterson. He had "looked at its charred ruins, its flooded streets, read its past in Nelson's history of Paterson, read of the Dutch who settled it." Finally, true to the physician he was, he took Paterson as "my 'case' to work up" and began the poem which was to be new "in the sense that in the very lay of syllables Paterson as Paterson would be discovered, perfect, perfect in the special sense of the poem, to have it—if it rose to flutter into life awhile—it would be as itself, locally, and so like every other place in the world. For it is in that, that it be particular to its own idiom, that it lives. The Falls let out a roar as it crashed upon the rocks at its base. In the imagination this roar is a speech or a voice, a speech in particular; it is the poem itself that is the answer."

At the end of Book Four the protagonist comes out of the sea where the Passaic has become undifferentiated, deathly, nothing particular, and he walks ashore with his "Chesapeake Bay Retriever," inland towards Walt Whitman's last home, Camden— Whitman in whose prosodic and humane footsteps Williams explicitly followed. But it was not so much the iambic meter-breaking that disturbed him, as the reception of the prose passages— letters, quotations from local history and geography in books and newspapers. It worried him perhaps more than it should have done. You soon grow used to the convention of his structure of prose and verse. Williams' reply to the critics' petty complaints appears in a 1948 letter to Parker Tyler:

> Prose and verse are both *writing*, both a matter of the words and an interrelation between words for the purpose of exposition, or other better defined purpose of *the art*. . . . Poetry does not *have* to be kept away from prose as Mr. Eliot might insist, it goes *along with* prose and, companionably, . . . by *itself* for what it is. It *belongs* there, in the gutter. Not anywhere else or wherever it is, it is the same: the poem.

But even in 1950, when he knew pretty well what he was doing in *Paterson*, Williams was still pressed for time. He tried to finish Book Four in the artists' colony at Saratoga Springs—"without this period of concentration I don't know how I should have been able to complete the task for another year." In 1951, in a letter to Marianne Moore, which is prefigured earlier in a letter to Babette Deutsch, after discussing her criticism of the "Corydon & Phyllis" sections of part four, he speaks of his "failure" to conclude the poem:

> If the vaunted purpose of my poem seems to fall apart at the end —it's rather frequent that one has to admit an essential failure . . . If I did not achieve a language I at least stated what I would not say. I would not melt myself into the great universal sea (of love) with all its shapes and colors. But, if I did not succeed on one level, I did cling to a living language on another. The poem, as opposed to what was accomplished in the story, came to life at moments—even when my failure was not most vocal and went above that to a different sort of achievement. Or so I believe. But maybe there's still another level on which I failed. If so, instruct me.

Williams' problem was to find a way of concluding part four without closing down his poem and the life in it, and without forcing the poetic experience into preconceived orders of either ideology or literature. "The Run to the Sea" must not be a cheap run home: "The sea is not our home." There is to be no relinquishing of the particular man, Paterson, to the generalized archetypes of the mythological sea, the sea of Jung or Eliot or Hart Crane: "Put wax rather in your ears against the hungry sea." Paterson, the compassionate democrat, is still an individual man, and the measure in the final paragraphs records the firmness of his emergence, with his "compact bitch," from the "filthy Passaic." He sleeps on the hot sand, dresses himself again in his working man's clothes, listens to the roar of the water, eats some wild fruit, and heads inland. Williams parallels this action with a newspaper report of a man hanged in 1850 on Garret Mountain —a real death, not a mythical or a mystical one with overtones of vague rebirth. Book Four, and the whole structure that Williams concluded here, ends with an ideogram of recurrent violence and recurrent vitality, and a theory of history which accommodates these without dehumanizing them:

> This is the blast
> the eternal close
> the spiral
> the final somersault
> the end.

To Marianne Moore, Williams wrote: "We all share the world together, we none of us possess it ourselves. We WANT to share it. Only because we are thwarted do we fail to achieve our release. But as poets all we can do is to say what we see and let the rest speak for itself."

Already in 1952, though, Williams felt a further book was needed, extending *Paterson* with his own life. The structure was so much the ordering of his own experience into a vision of art, science and love, that his own old age could be the natural and necessary closure of *Paterson*. In Book Five, Paterson is more nearly the poem. The older poet finds that he has his past still to learn and review; he feels the future through a brilliant young poet whose first book he had introduced and who represents the recurrence of having to suffer in order to come to terms with the city and the river and the sea. And more than this, Williams was still perfecting his line as part of his "assertion of artistic inde-pendence . . . based on the universal community of art" (John C. Thirlwall, "Two Cities: Paris and Paterson," *Massachusetts Review*, Winter 1962). He must, he writes to Sister Bernetta Quinn, go beyond the measures of Eliot and Pound:

I want to make the new meter out of whole cloth, I've got to know the necessity back of it. I don't want to appear in person. But I want to see the unknown shine, like a sunrise. I want to see that overpowering mastery that will inundate the whole scene, penetrate to that last jungle. It can be detected in the remote province of a Paterson as well as elsewhere.

But this "blessed rage for order" is tempered, as it always is in Williams, with an urgent respect for the facts of strictly human existence:

A man must, without relinquishing any of the reasons for the poetry with which he surrounds himself and with which the great of this world, at their most powerful, surround him, fight his way to a world which breaks through to the actual.

He goes on to say (to Ralph Nash in 1954) that this has always been his concern and always stands between him and Pound. All form and theory have had to knuckle down to the facts:

I knew most of the people with which I was in one way or other concerned, and that filled my eyes and my brain and allowed no room for anything else. (to Henry Wells, 1955)

So he had to work out and maintain his own persistent linear form. Both in a letter to John C. Thirlwall in 1954 and in the *Paris Review* interview in 1962, he declares that his "solution to the problem of modern verse," his "experiment in the variable foot," appears in Book Two—between "The descent beckons / as the ascent beckoned . . ." and "a descent follows, / endless and indestructible." (Williams reprinted this passage as "The Descent" at the beginning of *The Desert Music and Other Poems,* 1954.) The particular movement of this early passage was to be the basis of *Paterson* Book Five and it is a curiously elusive prosody to describe properly. This is partly because of its simplicity and aptness, and partly because a way of discussing prosody adequately is still being invented. In an extremely useful essay, which ought to be published as soon as possible, Lionel Kearns, the Canadian poet and linguist, discusses what he calls "stacked-verse." This is not only the method of his own poetry, but it also enables him to suggest some theoretical possibilities of handling prosodic description which are outstandingly sensible.

Olson's and Duncan's organic form and William's variable foot Kearns finds as vague terms in which to talk of "measure"—that is, the structure of "rhetorical stress." He puts his finger on the central problem which urged Williams to work out his own final line, the problem of poetic notation—the need, especially clear in contemporary stress-verse, to decide where the lines end and why, the relationship of the oral poem to the same poem printed for reading, and of the poem the poet may present in a public reading and the poem whose form we know from the page. Williams, when reading his poems on records, does not invariably make the printed structure of his measure appear in his voice cadences, rhythms and silences. This is primarily because speech —his own speech, American speech, New Jersey and Manhattan speech—is his basis: "I wanted to say something in a certain tone of my voice which would be exactly how I wanted to say it, to measure it in a certain way." At this stage, in 1962, he emphasized "what you encounter on the page" as what "must be transcribed to the page from the lips of the poet, as it was in such a master as Sappho." And he adds: *"The Descent* was very important to me in that way." The measure is to imitate the poet and, in a truly Aristotelian sense, is the structural form of a mimesis. It is neither "free verse" nor "vers libre." It is not "just to please the ear" but is to have a "total effect" and is to "read regularly." Williams did not work onwards from theory, although in a sense his foundation was the urge to make a local American poetic speech. He admitted to Stanley Koehler that he was in fact "almost manic" when he wrote the "Descent" passage—"excited" but not "conscious of doing anything unusual":

> I realized that something had occurred to me, which was a very satisfying conclusion to my poetic process. Something happened to my line that completed it, completed the rhythm, or at least it was satisfying to me. It was still an irregular composition; but not too much so.

But if artistic independence was maintained here, with a degree of regularity, it was still "too regular" for Williams at the end of his life: "there were certain variations of mood which would have led me to make a different poem out of it." In fact the variations of mood and the varieties of rhythmic invention in Book Five of *Paterson* and throughout the three books of *Pictures from Brueghel* (1954 to 1962) are an extraordinary achievement in exploring the possibilities of stress-verse, a measure whose variety of poises between the regularity and the impulsive freedom of speech is, with the measures in the *Cantos*, the major source of English poetic instruction today. Williams and Pound can show us how to organize a poem as "field of action."

II

In *The Great American Novel* (1923) Williams criticized the pretentiousness of this particularly nationalist pretence—a national epic novel—and hits out at traditional forms of large order:

> Permanence. A great army with its tail in antiquity.
> Cliché of the soul's beauty . . .

But if the plot of *Paterson* was to be, as Hugh Kenner puts it in an essay in his *Gnomon*, "the systematic eschewal both of pseudo-Aristotelian plot with its stereotyped climax, and of pseudo-Roman fine writing with its spurious epithets and cadences," what kind of response does the *Paterson* plot yield? Like Whitman, Williams refused to let an epic structure be the metaphor of the past as a European past or any kind of non-American past in the manner of the *Cantos* or the *Four Quartets*. But the metaphorical complexity of *The Bridge*, the Mississippi basin mysticism of Sandburg, and the theoretical analysis of pleasure and "poverty" in *Notes Toward a Supreme Fiction* and *Esthétique du Mal* were equally repugnant to his sensibility. *Paterson* is not a metaphor of anything else. To use Hugh Kenner again, "the poem was respectfully, enthusiastically received, and in unexpected quarters. But it isn't a metaphor, it isn't 'about' *something else* (Europe—the past); so it seems undiscussable, except via 'the inadequacy of Imagism' or some such trodden detour." In writing down the facts selected to show what happens and how it is, the poem is continually, for the reader, "in touch with something dense, not something that the writer has densified by mixing quick-drying ideas with it." The order of *Paterson* is not shored-up ruins which somehow lead to religious conversion; nor is it the ideogrammatically layered comparison of civilizations which are intended to yield aesthetic and moral relativities: "not a great order smashed but a new one so far voiceless." And this order is a human community, continually there in its reciprocities between Williams and the actuality of things and people known at first hand. *Paterson* contains no doctrinaire pronouncements, methodological keys such as personae, ideograms, objective correlatives, masks and so on, or proclamations of radical impersonality. It is not, to use Edwin Honig's words in his useful article, "That Mutation of Pound's," *Kenyon Review* (Summer 1955), "besieged by erudition." It is unlike Frost's offensively squirearchical agrarian community poetry with its basis in laissez-faire capitalist indecision and madness. Williams' poetic process is that of the Curies' discovery in Book Four:

> A dissonance
> in the valence of Uranium
> led to the discovery
>
> Dissonance
> (if you're interested)
> leads to discovery
>
> —to dissect away
> the block and leave
> a separate metal:
>
> hydrogen
> the flame, helium the
> pregnant ash.
>
> —the elephant takes two years

This is why Roy Harvey Pearce is mistaken when he remarks that "the strictly historical materials in *Paterson* are presented as so much *disjecta membra* and are allowed to have meaning only as they fit into the poet's scheme of things (which is the situation of *The Waste Land*)" (*The Continuity of American Poetry*, p. 336). But it is Eliot who fits his materials into his scheme: the quality of local Western life matters for him finally only if it makes a criticism of the absence of Christian dogma and a Tory-Monarchist class society in which the best life is the village life under a local triumvirate of church, manor and "significant soil." When Pearce also says "things are not objects for [Williams], nor are the men *dramatis personae*," again one must disagree with a critic whose standards are symbolist and traditional in Eliot's sense. Williams' people are people he has known, not *dramatis personae* or metaphors in a preconceived plot, itself the metaphor of a cosmic or ideological plot. Williams is neither Christian nor agrarian nor Marxist. His intuition of 1945 was correct: Dewey's instrumentalism could have helped him, as *Art as Experience* can show.

In 1927, like many of his contemporaries, Williams protested against the conduct of the Sacco and Vanzetti trial. One result was his "Impromptu: The Suckers," an attack on exploiters of the working class. The same year he began notes for "a big serious portrait of my time." In *New Directions*, 1937, he published *Paterson Episode 17*, some of the fragments he was building into a poem (they appear later in Book Three section three). Gradually this social, personal and committed poem grew into a shaped, hard-won whole, and central was the Passaic falls—the example of speech in a language in motion controlled by stress. But as Williams wrote in a publisher's release in 1951 (quoted by Thirlwall: William Carlos Williams' *Paterson—New Directions 17*, 1961): "I had to think hard how I was going to end the poem. It wouldn't do to have a grand and soul-satisfying conclusion, because I didn't see any in my subject." The natural conclusion was to be the vision of vital continuities in old age in Book Five—not a conventional serenity or the exasperating "wisdom of old age" racket, but simply new experience which accrues to an old wise man in his ultimate days.

Williams said a number of times outside his poem what *Paterson* was intended to be about, but most especially in a 1949 summary and in the blurb to the single volume edition of Books One to Four. Paterson is a man and in himself a city, "beginning, seeking, achieving and concluding his life in ways which the var-

ious aspects of a city may embody—if imaginatively conceived—
any city." In 1958, when he was seventy-five, Williams published
Book Five and wrote to his publisher: "I have been forced to
recognize that there may be no end to such a story as I have envisioned with the terms which I have laid down for myself. I had
to take the world of Paterson into a new dimension if I wanted
to give it imaginative validity." So finally he leaves the Passaic,
the city and the ocean of death and moves to The Cloisters museum, the European Romanesque church in upper New York, high
above the Hudson River, from where he can contemplate his age
and in which he can contemplate the fourteenth and fifteenth
century French tapestries of the Lady and the Unicorn, and
meditate in the new alert calm of old age the survival of men in
great art—not in ideology but in the action of art.

Central in Book One is the dramatization of divorce and division between life and anti-life, between ideologists or ideological
canned-goods men, as Saul Bellow might say, and the healing,
integrating powers of life in a common language which tries to
delineate observation and incident into an epiphany of that life
—"Say it, no ideas but in things"—"To make a start, / out of
particulars"—"What common language to unravel?" Paterson
the man is chained by the industrial exploitation program, de-
scended from Alexander Hamilton and now demonstrated in the
hydro-electric plant of the SUM (Society for Useful Manufac-
tures). Industrial capitalism divorces human energy from life
purpose and exhausts as it exploits directed energy. In a letter to
the protagonist, a poetess detects the divorce of poet from man
in him; a series of newspaper items expose forms of division and
abnormality, monstrousness, futile action and the failure of
language. The universities are accused of failing to unify into a
new whole the mass of inherited learning which instead is sterile,
as divorced from the people as the artist.

In Book Two, Garret Mountain park is the scene of the vul-
garity and breakdown in the sexual, religious and family life of
the city, of the Paterson workers in their Sunday leisure time.
Their lives are thin, as blocked as the woman describes in her
letter—"that kind of blockage exiling one's self from one's self,"
and "walking indifferent through / each other's privacy." This is
a society in which Eisenstein's "Que Viva Mexico!", a film fully
imagining the continuity of life, is suppressed. Usury and SUM
pollute the Passaic, and all the park preacher can do is preach,
in monstrous opposition, the dogma of heavenly riches—"beauty

— / torn to shreds by the / lurking schismatists." The springtime
renewal and initiation urge "beckons to new places'" out of "the
death of all that's past." But the poet, who "seeks to induce his
bones to rise into a scene, / his dry bones, above the scene," is
sterile. Marriage and a new language are urgently needed now in
order to combat empty knowledge, worn-out and wasted words.
The poet must reject the voice urging him to "be reconciled with
your world," Paterson and his woman separate: she cries "You
have abandoned me" and he flees "pursued by the roar" of the
waters. A short sensuous lyrical section then suggests how true
reconciliation might be:

> On this most voluptuous night of the year
> the term of the moon is yellow with no light
> the air's soft, the night bird has
> only one note, the cherry tree in bloom
>
> makes a blur on the woods, its perfume
> no more than half guessed moves in the mind . . .

But Book Two ends with a long letter of despair from the
poetess criticizing Dr. Paterson, among other things, for his attitudes towards the social purpose of poetry.

Book Three opens with the contrast between the cool white
beauty of the locust tree in June and the heavy weight of books
in the public library, cool in the summer but a place of "desolation" too: "it has a smell of its own / of stagnation and death."
The library is countered by the vitality of the locust tree, the
stars in the sky, and a naked patient of Dr. Paterson's who, as
poet, is now tempted to give up writing *Paterson*, to stop trying
to be a saint who believes in "this swill-hole of corrupt cities."
Toulouse-Lautrec is mentioned as the example of monstrousness
and division who yet made a language and an art out of squalor
and apparent sterility—"a poetry / of the movements of cost,
known and unknown." The painter-hero-dwarf is the articulator
of the city to whom Williams will dedicate *Paterson* Book Five.
But now the protagonist allows the library flames to consume him,
overwhelm and intoxicate him, because he refuses to be one of
those in whom fires "smoulder a lifetime and never burst / into
flame." The flaming library is beauty in "defiance of authority,"
the opposite of Dürer's engraving of Melancholy which illustrates
desolation caused by "the mathematics of the machine": "vul-
garity of beauty" surpasses the perfections of analytical learning.

The "beautiful thing" resists division; the poem resists trash and the emptiness of the glittering surfaces of the past. Beauty shapes after it has shaken the man, and it must include the scarred legs of the whipped child with the torn unicorn and the queenly lady in those great tapestries which will be the focus of Book Five. But above all, beauty is the girl who concludes this section— "flame, / black plush, a dark flame."

The world's survival depends on accuracy, especially on the accuracy of language, and therefore section three concerns the clearing of debris after destruction, the flooding Passaic leading to new life. The lines of the poem break into fragmentary forms in a visual diagram of ruin and rebirth. The poet of necessary eccentricity is Pound—his famous epistolary manner, his desperately abnormal reading list. But this is ideogrammatically checked by a list of well borings reaching down to a point at 2100 feet where water is "altogether unfit for ordinary use," followed by a criticism of the "insane engineer" Eliot which this article has already quoted. Williams also includes Hart Crane's attack on Eliot:

> Loosen the flesh
> from the machine, build no more
> bridges.   Through what air will you
> fly to span the continents?

Williams then speaks of his own poem:

> I must
> find my meaning and lay it, white
> beside the sliding water: myself—
> comb out the language—or succumb
>
> —whatever the complexion. Let
> me out!   (Well, go!) this rhetoric
> is real!

After destruction and violence, Book Four is a steady run to the deathly sea. Dr. Paterson's own mock-pastoral love affair competes with an amusing, tender but difficult affair between two women—an extraordinarily complex short story in verse and prose. The tunnel under the Passaic is given a Dante reference to Hell, but this is a real city hell, and not a hell for the lovers because their poetry is "news" and their relationship an example

of alert form within the chaos of predatory living. A lecture on
atomic fission is the example of division and destruction of rub-
bish in order to produce the metal of value, and it parallels the
poet's own destruction of old forms to produce the new measure
and structure. But Marie Curie's invention has results like Billy
Sunday's spurious evangelizing: her lonely research is paralleled
with the trials of a young poet living in Paterson, Allen Ginsberg,
who at this time was unknown. He refers in his letter, quoted
here, to poems later published in *Empty Mirror* and to the genesis
of the beat generation writers as they strive for renewal of form
in opposition to the city hell of the late 1940s. Ginsberg connects
Pierre and *The Confidence-Man* with Jack Kerouac's experiments
in prose and describes his own poetic aims, his sense of actually
living in the city of Williams' poem, his sense of the "splendor"
of the free spirit he carries within himself in 1946, his acceptance
of "no ideas but in things," and his own work as "clear statement
of fact about misery." (Williams introduces *Howl* as exactly such
a poem in 1956, and this is referred to in Book Five.)

The ideogram of dissonance and discovery in science, love and
poetry continues as the protagonist recalls the anguish and poverty of student life, of Villon at the age of thirty, of Columbus—
all examples of "luminous" quality in a world governed by money.
Uranium may be the beginning of a cancer cure, but what is the
cure for the social cancer of high finance of capitalism's usury?
Money is a criminal joke, actually causing squalor. Credit, like
uranium, should be for social use—even the Southern Fugitives
made their 1931 "stand" against the right enemy at least.

Then the protagonist returns to his own purposes—to give birth
to language and the poem before he is too old. He recalls the in-
scription on an ashtray gift: "La Vertue / est toute dans l'effort,"
and places this beside the words of a whore whom he had loved:
"virtue . . . is a stout old bird, unpredictable." This paring is
evolved into one of Williams' central dialectics—virtue of virgin
purpose and virtue of whore's love, a love which is central to
Book Five and which, here, is the ultimate human virtue, the
capability of love: "a fragrance / of mown hay, facing the rapa-
cious, / the 'great'." Now the *upper* Passaic is celebrated—the
loveliness of natural landscape, colonial peace between Indian and
Dutch settler, colonial quality of applied arts, colonial community
—and sharply juxtaposed to contemporary city and river con-
tempt for exactly these ideals, excellently defined as "a poverty of

resource." The ultimate poverty is war, specifically the Pacific War of the 1940s, the extreme case of divorce and division, like "the shark, that snaps / at his own trailing guts, makes a sunset / of the green water," an image to which Williams referred in a letter to Jose Garcia Villa in 1950:

> A cold east wind, today, that seems to blow from the other side of the world—seems at the same time to be blowing all poetry out of life. A man wonders why he bothers to continue to write. And yet it is precisely then that to write is most imperative for us. That, if I can do it, will be the end of *Paterson*, Book IV. The ocean of savage lusts in which the wounded shark gnashes at his own tail is not our home.
>
> It is the seed that floats to shore, one word, one tiny, even microscopic word, is that which can alone save us.

Paterson resists the fashionable myth of the sea as origin and home, the false nostalgia of "vain regrets." It is better, like Ulysses' sailors, to wax up your ears against the sea temptations. The future comes from the sea as "the seed of Venus . . . a girl standing upon a tilted shell, rose/pink," but only to the wanderer who can swim in the sea, come ashore, sleep and finally, in his faded working overalls, head inland. The closing rhythms are quiet and confident, the movement of firm survival without nostalgia for old ideologies and religions.

Book Five opens with Paterson in old age, a confident eagle, still rebellious, remembering the earlier city and river, remembering early Spring, the love of Lorca's old Don Perlimplin for the young girl and of Dante for his child-beloved, Beatrice. The virgin's maidenhead is like the singleness which has to be overcome by necessary violence of sexual love in order to ensure fertility. Artists and poets celebrate that fertility. High above New York, on the "rock-ridge" of Fort Tryon Park, the poet meditates the transcendent transformations and permanence of art: "A WORLD OF ART / THAT THROUGH THE YEARS HAS / SURVIVED! / —the museum become real." The principle of the "beautiful thing" and "no idea but in things" is consummated in the tapestries of the Lady and the Unicorn in The Cloisters museum. The unicorn, which the first recorder of the legend, Ctesias, says cannot be overtaken by any other beast, the wild and unconquerable beast of vital energy, is caught, so the myth holds, only by the virgin, in whose lap he lays his head. In this state he is easily held by the hunter. Williams uses this construction on the myth and not the Christian medieval allegory of unicorn, lady and hunter as Christ, Mary and Gabriel. But he also uses the plants, over a hundred varieties in the tapestries, and allows the spring flowers and the beasts to recall Audubon's recording of American nature. This natural life surrounds the death of the matchless creature, and the tapestry defeats even his death by being permanently the action of imaginative beauty.

Allen Ginsberg features here again as a young man still working to articulate his experience in the Passaic world, and he is placed with the enduring art of Jackson Pollock and Ben Shahn. Gauguin, dying of syphilis from a whore, ironically presents the risks of love for the artist, of being trapped by the Virgin. A translation of a lyric by Sappho, a letter from Pound (still arguing against usura, still trying to educate the young), a lesbian trying to work out her life in Paterson, a passage from Mezzrow's *Really the Blues* recalling the truth of Bessie Smith's music—this sequence leads to a superb long passage on the destructive element in art. In the satyr-play's dancing "all the deformities take wing": Klee, Picasso and Gris, Dürer, Leonardo and Bosch are the examples of artistic distortion and deformity made into enduring art, an art of loving redemption which is compared to that same Jew whom Schöenberg celebrated in *A Survivor from Warsaw*, who was "comforting his companions" whilst buried among them. Only the beasts are "blameless."

In section three, the protagonist sees himself as a midwife, or like Dr. Williams, bringing many children into the world: "imagination must be served— / and he served / dispassionately." Old Paterson comforts himself with the marvellous tapesteries, with Chaucer's poetry of birds, and with the birds themselves. Then, through a childhood memory of his uncle Godwin, who died young and insane, killing a snake, he presents—more like Williams himself now—the great emblem of the *ouroboros*, the serpent with its tail in its mouth, the image of life returning to its origins, the river returning to its springs, the sign of endless life and the renewal *in life* of human wisdom.

The last six pages are a structure of faith in human life. "The times are not heroic" since Paterson began, "but they are clearer / and freer of disease." The heroic tapestries present both the anguish and the fulfilment of love and energy to Paterson, now "the King-self," incarnated in the seventh tapestry of the unicorn wounded, alive, experienced, magnificent:

```
         —the hunt of
            the Unicorn and
                the god of love
         of virgin birth
            The mind is the demon
            drives us . . .
```

The simple loveliness of the flowers around this heroic emblematic action recall the beauty of the locust tree in Book Three and the beauty of all the women in the poem, examples of eternal womanhood, accompanied by the necessary young lover "sharing the female world / in Hell's despight graciously." The poet's grandmother proclaims "the past is for those that lived in the past" and the poet himself makes a final calm intelligent claim for the one knowledge he is certain of—the shaping poetic measure, the new, the dance. It is not a question of either knowing nothing or assuming that existence is a chess game of determinism:

```
         We know nothing and can know nothing.
                  but
         the dance, to dance to a measure
         contrapuntally,
                  Satyrically, the tragic foot.
```

As Williams affirmed in his interview with Koehler, *Paterson* concludes with this image of "energy within form," a dance-action which he associated with the Indians of America, the first men of Paterson, a real origin rather than a spurious religious myth of eternal return.

The notes for a projected Book Six which Williams made in January 1961 contain very little but it is at least clear that his sensibility worked around examples of the kind he needed to reinforce, repeat and augment the poem's central concerns: men from the American past (Madison, Jay, Hamilton, Washington), the theme of wasted life and wasted money, the dance which releases and controls egoism, Sappho's poems lost in the library of Alexandria, and the bitter humiliation of "the pure products of America." Williams still felt the urge to complete his "little universe," as much as Faulkner did his postage stamp plot of Southern ground. But "complete" is hardly the right word. *Paterson*, in its own nature, is not to be completed and the two "conclusions" and the final notes for a further book indicate the identification of the poem with a man's composing life. The *Cantos*

are Pound; *Paterson* is Williams. His motives for *Paterson* even-
tually sustained him over the twenty years of its composition:
"Any poem that has worth expresses the whole life of the poet.
It gives a view of what the poet is."

Randall Jarrell

[Dr. Williams' *Paterson*]

I

Paterson (Book I) seems to me the best thing William Carlos
Williams has ever written; I read it seven or eight times, and
ended lost in delight. It is a shame to write a little review of
it, instead of going over it page by page, explaining and admir-
ing. And one hates to quote much, since the beauty, delicacy,
and intelligence of the best parts depend so much upon their
organization in the whole; quoting from it is like humming a
theme and expecting a hearer to guess from that its effect upon
its third repetition in a movement. I have used this simile deliber-
ately, because—over and above the organization of argument or
exposition—the organization of *Paterson* is musical to an almost
unprecedented degree: Dr. Williams introduces a theme that
stands for an idea, repeats it over and over in varied forms, develops it side by side with two or three more themes that are
being developed, recurs to it time and time again throughout the
poem, and echoes it for ironic or grotesque effects in thoroughly
incongruous contexts. Sometimes this is done with the greatest
complication and delicacy; he wants to introduce a bird whose call
will stand for the clear speech of nature, in the midst of all the
confusion and ugliness in which men could not exist except for
"imagined beauty where there is none"; so he says in disgust,
"Stale as a whale's breath: breath! / Breath!" and ten lines later
(during which three themes have been repeated and two of them

From *Poetry and the Age,* copyright 1953 by Randall Jarrell, pp. 226-233,
260-265. Reprinted by permission of Alfred A. Knopf, Inc.

joined at last in a "silent, uncommunicative," and satisfying reso-
lution) he says that he has

> Only of late, late! begun to know, to
> know clearly (as through clear ice) whence
> I draw my breath or how to employ it
> clearly—if not well:
> > Clearly!
> speaks the red-breast his behest. Clearly!
> clearly!

These double exclamations have so prepared for the bird's call
that it strikes you, when you are reading the poem itself, like
the blow which dissolves an enchantment. And really the preparation has been even more complicated: two pages before there
was the line "divorce! divorce!" and, half a page before, the birds
and weeds by the river were introduced with

> . . . white, in
> the shadows among the blue-flowered
> Pickerel-weed, in summer, summer! if it should
> ever come . . .

If you want to write a long poem which doesn't stick to one
subject, but which unifies a dozen, you can learn a good deal from
Paterson.

The subject of *Paterson* is: How can you tell the truth about
things?— that is, how can you find a language so close to the
world that the world can be represented and understood in it?

> Paterson lies in the valley under the Passaic Falls
> its spent waters forming the outline of his back. He
> lies on his right side, head near the thunder
> of the water filling his dreams! Eternally asleep,
> his dreams walk about the city where he persists
> incognito. Butterflies settle on his stone ear.

How can he—this city that is man—find the language for what
he sees and is, the language without which true knowledge is
impossible? He starts with the particulars ("Say it, no ideas but
in things") which stream to him like the river, "rolling up out
of chaos, / a nine months' wonder"; with the interpenetration

of everything with everything, "the drunk the sober; the illustrious / the gross; one":

> It is the ignorant sun
> rising in the slot of
> hollow suns risen, so that never in this
> world will a man live well in his body
> save dying—and not know himself
> dying . . .

The water falls and then rises in "floating mists, to be rained
down and / regathered into a river that flows / and encircles";
the water, in its time, is "combed into straight lines / from that
rafter of a rock's / lip," and attains clarity; but the people are
like flowers that the bee misses, they fail and die and "Life is
sweet, they say"—but their speech has failed them, "they do
not know the words / or have not / the courage to use them,"
and they hear only "a false language pouring—a / language (mis-
understood) pouring (misinterpreted) without / dignity, without minister, crashing upon a stone ear." And the language
available to them, the language of scholarship and science and
the universities, is

> a bud forever green
> tight-curled, upon the pavement, perfect
> in justice and substance but divorced, divorced
> from its fellows, fallen low—
> >   Divorce is
> the sign of knowledge in our time,
> divorce! divorce!

Girls walk by the river at Easter and one, bearing a willow
twig in her hand as Artemis bore the moon's crescent bow,

> holds it, the gathered spray,
> upright in the air, the pouring air,
> strokes the soft fur—
> >   Ain't they beautiful!

(How could words show better than these last three the touching
half-success, half-failure of their language?) And Sam Patch, the
professional daredevil who jumped over the Falls with his pet
bear, could *say* only: "Some things can be done as well as others";

and Mrs. Cumming, the minister's wife, shrieked unheard and
fell unseen from the brink; and the two were only

> : a body found next spring
> frozen in an ice-cake; or a body
> fished next day from the muddy swirl—
>
> both silent, uncommunicative.

The speech of sexual understanding, of natural love, is represented
by three beautifully developed themes: a photograph of the nine
wives of a Negro chief; a tree standing on the brink of a waterfall;
and two lovers talking by the river:

> We sit and talk and the
> silence speaks of the giants
> who have died in the past and have
> returned to those scenes unsatisfied
> and who is not unsatisfied, the
> silent, Singac the rock-shoulder
> emerging from the rocks—and the giants
> live again in your silence and
> unacknowledged desire . . .

But now the air by the river "brings in the rumors of separate
worlds," and the poem is dragged from its highest point in the
natural world, from the early, fresh, and green years of the city,
into the slums of Paterson, into the collapse of this natural
language, into a "delirium of solutions," into the back streets
of that "great belly / that no longer laughs but mourns / with
its expressionless black navel love's / deceit." Here is the whole
failure of Paterson's ideas and speech, and he is forced to begin
all over; Part II of the poem ends with the ominous, "No ideas
but / in the facts."

Part III opens with this beautiful and unexpected passage.

> How strange you are, you idiot!
> So·you think because the rose
> is red that you shall have the mastery?
> The rose is green and will bloom,
> overtopping you, green, livid
> green when you shall no more speak, or
> taste, or even be. My whole life
> has hung too long upon a partial victory.

The underlying green of the facts always cancels out the red
in which we had found our partial, temporary, aesthetic victory;
and the poem now introduces the livid green of the obstinate
and contorted lives, the lifeless perversions of the industrial city.
Here are the slums; here is the estate with its acre hothouse,
weedlike orchids, and French maid whose only duty is to "groom /
the pet Pomeranians—who sleep"; here is the university with
its clerks

> spilled on fixed concepts like
> roasting hogs, sputtering, their drip sizzling in the fire
>
> Something else, something else the same.

Then (in one of the fine prose quotations—much altered by the
poet, surely—which interrupt the verse) people drain the lake
there, all day and all night long kill the fish and eels with clubs,
carry them away in baskets; there is nothing left but the mud.
The sleeping Paterson, "moveless," envies the men who could
run off "toward the peripheries—to other centers, direct," for
some "loveliness and / authority in the world," who could leap
like Sam Patch and be found "the following spring, frozen in /
an ice cake." But he goes on thinking to a very bitter end, and
reproduces the brutal ignorance of his city as something both
horrible and pathetic:

> And silk spins from the hot drums to a music
> of pathetic souvenirs, a comb and nail-file
> in an imitation leather case—to
> remind him, to remind him! and
> a photograph-holder with pictures of himself
> between the two children, all returned
> weeping, weeping—in the back room
> of the widow who married again, a vile tongue
> but laborious ways, driving a drunken
> husband . . .

But he contrasts his own mystery, the mystery of people's actual
lives, with the mystery that "the convent of the Little Sisters of /
St. Ann pretends"; and he understands the people "wiping the
nose on sleeves, come here / to dream"; he understands that

> Things, things unmentionable
> the sink with the waste farina in it and
> lumps of rancid meat, milk-bottle-tops: have
> here a still tranquillity and loveliness . . .

Then Paterson "shifts his change," and an earthquake and a "remarkable rumbling noise" frighten the city but leave it undamaged—this in the prose of an old newspaper account; and at the end of the poem he stands in the flickering green of the cavern under the waterfall (the dark, skulled world of consciousness), hedged in by the pouring torrent whose thunder drowns out any language: "The myth / that holds up the rock, / that holds up the water thrives there— / in that cavern, that profound cleft"; and the readers of the poem have shown to them, in the last words of the poem,

> standing, shrouded there, in that din,
> Earth, the chatterer, father of all
> speech . . . .

It takes several readings to work out the poem's argument (it is a poem that *must* be read over and over), and it seemed to me that I could do most for its readers by roughly summarizing that argument. There are hundreds of things in the poem that deserve specific mention. The poem is weakest in the middle of the third section—I'd give page numbers if New Directions had remembered to put any in—but this seems understandable and almost inevitable. Everything in the poem is interwoven with everything else, just as the strands of the Falls interlace: how wonderful and unlikely that this extraordinary mixture of the most delicate lyricism of perception and feeling with the hardest and homeliest actuality should ever have come into being! There has never been a poem more American (though the only influence one sees in it is that of the river scene from *Finnegans Wake*); if the next three books are as good as this one, which introduces "the elemental character of the place," the whole poem will be the best very long poem that any American has written.

II

Paterson (Book I) seemed to me a wonderful poem; I should not have supposed beforehand that William Carlos Williams could do the organizing and criticizing and selecting that a work of this length requires. Of course, Book I is not organized quite so well as a long poem *ought* to be, but this is almost a defining characteristic of long poems—and I do not see how anyone could do better using only those rather mosaic organizational techniques that Dr. Williams employs, and neglecting as much as he does narrative, drama, logic, and sustained movement, the primary

organizers of long poems. I waited for the next three books of
Paterson more or less as you wait for someone who has gone to
break the bank at Monte Carlo for the second, third, and fourth
times; I was afraid that I knew what was going to happen, but
I kept wishing as hard as I could that it wouldn't.

Now that Book IV has been printed, one can come to some
conclusions about *Paterson* as a whole. My first conclusion is
this: it doesn't seem to *be* a whole; my second: *Paterson* has
been getting rather steadily worse. Most of Book IV is much
worse than II and III, and neither of them even begins to compare with Book I. Book IV is so disappointing that I do not want
to write about it at any length: it would not satisfactorily conclude even a quite mediocre poem. Both form and content often
seem a parody of those of the "real" *Paterson;* many sections
have a scrappy inconsequence, an arbitrary irrelevance, that is
extraordinary; poetry of the quality of that in Book I is almost
completely lacking—though the forty lines about a new Odysseus
coming in from the sea are particularly good, and there are other
fits and starts of excellence. There are in Part III long sections
of a measure that sounds exactly like the stuff you produce when
you are demonstrating to a class that any prose whatsoever can
be converted into four-stress accentual verse simply by inserting
line-endings every four stresses. These sections *look* like blank
verse, but are flatter than the flattest blank verse I have ever
read—for instance: "Branching trees and ample gardens gave /
the village streets a delightful charm and / the narrow old-
fashioned brick walls added / a dignity to the shading trees. It
was a fair / resort for summer sojourners on their way / to the
Falls, the main object of interest." This passage suggests that
the guidebook of today is the epic of tomorrow; and a worse
possibility, the telephone book put into accentual verse, weighs
upon one's spirit.

Books II and III are much better than this, of course: Book
II is decidedly what people call "a solid piece of work," but
most of the magic is gone. And one begins to be very doubtful
about the organization: should there be so much of the evangelist
and his sermon? Should so much of this book consist of what
are—the reader is forced to conclude—real letters from a real
woman? One reads these letters with involved, embarrassed pity,
quite as if she had walked into the room and handed them to one.
What has been done to them to make it possible for us to respond
to them as art, not as raw reality? to make them part of the

poem *Paterson?* I can think of no answer except: "They have been copied out on the typewriter." Anyone can object, "But the context makes them part of the poem"; and anyone can reply to this objection, "It takes a lot of context to make somebody else's eight-page letter the conclusion to a book of a poem."

Book II introduces—how one's heart sinks!—Credit and Usury, those enemies of man, God, and contemporary long poems. Dr. Williams has always put up a sturdy resistance to Pound when Pound has recommended to him Santa Sophia or the Parthenon, rhyme or metre, European things like that; yet he takes Credit and Usury over from Pound and gives them a good home and maintains them in practically the style to which they have been accustomed—his motto seems to be, *I'll adopt your child if only he's ugly enough.* It is interesting to see how much some later parts of *Paterson* resemble in their structure some middle and later parts of the *Cantos*: the Organization of Irrelevance (or, perhaps, the Irrelevance of Organization) suggests itself as a name for this category of structure. Such organization is *ex post facto* organization: if something is somewhere, one can always find Some Good Reason for its being there, but if it had not been there would one reader have missed it? if it had been put somewhere else, would one reader have guessed where it should have "really" gone? Sometimes these anecdotes, political remarks, random comments seem to be where they are for one reason: because Dr. Williams chose—happened to choose—for them to be there. One is reminded of that other world in which Milton found Chance "sóle arbiter."

Book III is helped very much by the inclusion of "Beautiful Thing," that long, extremely effective lyric that was always intended for *Paterson*; and Book III, though neither so homogeneous nor so close to Book I, is in some respects superior to Book II. But all three later books are worse organized, more eccentric and idiosyncratic, more self-indulgent, than the first. And yet that is not the point, the real point: the *poetry*, the lyric rightness, the queer wit, the improbable and dazzling perfection of so much of Book I have disappeared—or at least, reappear only fitfully. Early in Book IV, while talking to his son, Dr. Williams quotes this to him: "What I miss, said your mother, is the poetry, the pure poem of the first parts." She is right.

I have written a good deal about Dr. Williams' unusual virtues, so I will take it for granted that I don't need to try to demonstrate, all over again, that he is one of the best poets alive. He was the last of the good poets of his generation to become properly appreciated; and some of his appreciators, in the blush of conversion, rather overvalue him now. When one reads that no "living American poet has written anything better and more ambitious" than *Paterson*, and that Dr. Williams is a poet who gives us "just about everything," one feels that the writer has in some sense missed the whole point of William Carlos Williams. He is a *very* good but *very* limited poet, particularly in vertical range. He is a notably unreasoning, intuitive writer—is not, of course, an intellectual in any sense of the word; and he has further limited himself by volunteering for and organizing a long dreary imaginary war in which America and the Present are fighting against Europe and the Past. But go a few hundred years back inside the most American American and it is Europe: Dr. Williams is just as much Darkest Europe as any of us, down there in the middle of his past.

In his long one-sided war with Eliot Dr. Williams seems to me to come off badly—particularly so when we compare the whole of *Paterson* with the *Four Quartets*. When we read the *Four Quartets* we are reading the long poem of a poet so temperamentally isolated that he does not even put another character, another human being treated at length, into the whole poem; and yet the poem (probably the best long poem since the *Duino Elegies*) impresses us not with its limitations but with its range and elevation, with how much it knows not simply about men but about Man—not simply about one city or one country but about the West, that West of which America is no more than the last part.

[Paterson I and II]

I

In a review that I imagine will become famous as an example of "the shock of recognition," Randall Jarrell has said about all that can be said in a short space of the construction of *Paterson*. I feel no embarrassment, however, for repeating, poorly but in different words, what has already been written. *Paterson* has made no stir either in the little magazines or in the commercial press; and yet I can think of no book published in 1946 that is as important, or of any living English or American poet who has written anything better or more ambitious. When it is completed, *Paterson* will run to over a hundred pages, and be in four parts. As only Book I has been published, the critic is faced with many uncertainties, and forced to make many conjectures.[1] Williams' own rather breathless and incoherent introductory note will, perhaps be of little help. "A man in himself is a city, beginning, seeking, achieving and concluding his life in the ways which the various aspects of the city may embody—if imaginatively conceived—any city, all the details of which may be made to voice his most intimate convictions." The poet begins with a slightly different statement of this purpose: "Rigor of beauty is the quest. But how will you find beauty when it is locked in the mind past all remonstrance?" The answer is "to make a start out of particulars . . . no ideas but in things." This may appear crude and vague, but Williams has nothing in common with the coarse, oratorical sentimentalists, most favorably represented by Carl Sandburg, who have written about cities and the people. More than any of his contemporaries, he resembles Wordsworth in his aims and values; and in its maturity, experience, and sympathy *Paterson* appears to me to be comparable to *The Prelude* and the opening of *The Excursion*.

From *Sewanee Review*, LV (1947), 500-3; and *Nation*, CLXVI (1948), 692-94. Reprinted by permission of the author and the original publisher. Copyright 1947, by the University of the South, and copyright 1948, by The Nation Associates, Inc.
[1]As the poem stands, it has many insufficiently related odds and ends. It is a defect perhaps that the human beings exist almost entirely in the prose passages.

I am not sure that I can say very clearly why, or even how it is that Williams' methods are successful. By personifying Paterson, and by "Patersonizing" himself, he is in possession of all the materials that he can use. First the City is his: all its aspects, its past, its present, its natural features, its population, and its activities are available for him to interrelate and make dramatic. But also he can use his whole life in the City—every detail is an experience, a memory, or a symbol. Taken together, Paterson is Williams' life, and Williams is what makes Paterson alive. For Williams, a man is what he experiences, and in his shorter lyrics he has perfected a technique of observation and of empathy. He can move from man outward: "The year plunges into night / and the heart plunges / lower than night / to an empty, wind-swept place / without sun, stars or moon / but a peculiar light as of thought / that spins a dark fire. . . ." Or the observed is personified: "Lifeless in appearance, sluggish / dazed spring approaches— / They enter the new world naked, / cold, uncertain of all / save that they enter." Which end he starts from matters little. Williams triumphs in his sense of motion, his ability to observe, and to fit his observations to the right rhythms.

But if the short poems show Williams as an excellent stylist, there is nothing in them to indicate that their thematic structure could be extended to a long poem. How this has been done and how *Paterson's* various themes are stated, developed, repeated, opposed, broken, and mingled, has been demonstrated at some length by Jarrell in *Partisan Review*. Here I shall confine myself to quoting passages in which the principal themes are expressed and to pointing out a few of their more important connections and meanings. The theme on which all the others depend is three-fold: a city—Paterson, New Jersey—, a mountain, and a river that flows from the mountain into Paterson—a man, a woman, and the man's thought. First the city:

Paterson lies in the valley under the Passaic Falls
its spent waters forming the outline of his back. He
lies on his right side, head near the thunder
of the waters filling his dreams! Eternally asleep
his dreams walk about the city where he persists
incognito. Butterflies settle on his stone ear.
Immortal he neither moves nor rouses and is seldom
seen, though he breathes and the subtleties of his machinations
drawing their substance from the noise of the pouring river
animate a thousand automatons.

The mountain is introduced in a parallel passage:

> And there, against him, stretches the low mountain.
> The Park's her head, carved above the Falls, by the quiet
> river; colored crystals the secret of those rocks;
> farms and ponds, laurel, and the temperate wild cactus,
> yellow flowered . . . facing him, his
> arm supporting her, by the *Valley of the Rocks*, asleep.
> Pearls at her ankles, her monstrous hair
> spangled with apple-blossoms is scattered about into
> the back country, waking their dreams—where the deer run
> and the wood-duck nests protecting his gallant plumage.

The passage introducing the river is too long to quote in full.

> Jostled as are the waters approaching
> the brink, his thoughts
> interlace, repel and cut under,
> rise rock-thwarted and turn aside
> but forever strain forward—or strike
> an eddy and whirl, marked by a
> leaf or curdy spume, seeming
> to forget. . . .

The Man-City and the Woman-Mountain are easier to understand than the river which symbolizes thought. It is the elemental thought that lacks a language, the source of life and motion. It is described again and again, always with such powerful precision that one is in no doubt of its grimness and strength. It is intercourse between Paterson and the mountain, and above all, it is Paterson's thoughts, his population—the primal vitality behind their lives and speech. The two lovers later meet under its falls, and in the prose records that are interspersed with the poetry, one reads of the men and women who were drowned in it, and the pearl and fish that were taken out of it. This threefold main-theme is repeated in smaller themes, such as the African chief with his seven wives on a log, and "the lightnings that stab at the mystery of a man from both ends." It is broken up in the two divorces: the university, "a bud forever green, / tight-curled, upon the pavement, perfect / in juice and substance but divorced, divorced / from its fellows, fallen low—"; and the "girls from / families that have decayed and / taken to the hills. . . . Life is sweet / they say: the language! / —the language / is divorced from their minds." "In ignorance a certain knowledge and knowledge, undispersed, its own undoing."

This is the tragedy of Paterson, what the poem is really about. It is the divorce of modern life, of intellect and sensibility, spirit and matter, and of the other stock categories that come to mind. His "quest for beauty" is a search for the whole man, whose faculties are harmonious, and whose language corresponds with the particulars and mystery of reality. Williams is liberal, anti-orthodox, and a descendant of Emerson and Whitman. But if a man is intense and honest enough, the half-truth of any extreme position will in time absorb much of its opposite. Williams has much in common with Catholic, aristocratic and Agrarian writers. For all his sympathy with his people, he makes one feel that the sword of Damocles hangs over Paterson, the modern city and world. As with Yeats, "things fall apart." The educated lack connection, and the ignorant are filled with speechless passion.

Williams has had much to say about Ezra Pound, one whom he may have envied for being able to "run off toward the peripheries to find loveliness and authority in the world—a sort of springtime toward which his mind aspired." Some of his pronouncements seemed unfair and hysterical, but in *Paterson* his position has paid off, when compared with Pound's. It is a sort of anti-Cantos rooted in America, in one city, and in what Williams has known long and seen often. Not only are its details enriched and verified by experience, but the whole has a unity that is analogous to the dramatic unities of time, place, and action. *Paterson* resembles *The Bridge;* but Hart Crane's poem, for all its splendor in its best moments, will not stand up to the comparison. It seems relatively inexperienced, chaotic and verbal. Even as a rhetorician Williams is much superior. It would be fruitless to compare *Paterson* with the best writing of Eliot, Stevens, Tate, or Auden, for the ways of writing very well are various; but for experience and observation, it has, along with a few poems of Frost, a richness that makes almost all other contemporary poetry look a little second-hand. If Books II, III, and IV are as good as Book I, *Paterson* will be the most successful really long poem since *The Prelude.*

II

Paterson, Book II, is an interior monologue. A man spends Sunday in the park at Paterson, New Jersey. He thinks and looks

about him; his mind contemplates, describes, comments, associates, stops, stutters, and shifts like a firefly, bound only by its
milieu. The man is Williams, anyone living in Paterson, the
American, the masculine principle—a sort of Everyman. His
monologue is interrupted by chunks of prose: paragraphs from
old newspapers, textbooks, and the letters of a lacerated and
lacerating poetess. This material is merely selected by the author.
That the poetry is able to digest it in the raw is a measure of
power and daring—the daring of simplicity; for only a taut style
with worlds of experience behind it could so resign, and give way
to the anthologist. The didactic chapters of *Moby-Dick* have a
similar function, and are the rock that supports the struggles
of Captain Ahab. The park is Everywoman, any woman, the
feminine principle, America. The water roaring down the falls
from the park to Paterson is the principle of life. The rock is
death, negation, the *nul*; carved and given form, it stands for
the imagination, "like a red basalt grasshopper, boot-long with
window-eyes." The symbols are not allegorical, but loose, intuitive, and Protean.

Paterson, like Hart Crane's "Marriage of Faustus and Helen,"
is about marriage. "Rigor of beauty is the quest." Everything in
the poem is masculine or feminine, everything strains toward
marriage, but the marriages never come off, except in the imagination, and there, attenuated, fragmentary, and uncertain. "Divorce is the sign of knowledge in our time." The people "reflect
no beauty but gross . . . unless it is beauty to be, anywhere, so
flagrant in desire." "The ugly legs of the young girls, pistons
without delicacy"; "not undignified"; "among the working classes
some sort of breakdown has occurred." The preacher in the
second section, attended by the "iron smiles" of his three middle-
aged disciples, by "benches on which a few children have been
propped by the others against their running off," "bends at the
knees and straightens himself up violently with the force of his
emphasis—like Beethoven getting a crescendo out of an orches-
tra"—ineffective, pathetic, and a little phony. He has given up;
or says he has given up, a fortune for the infinite riches of our
Lord Jesus Christ. Interspersed through his sermon, as an ironic
counter-theme, is Alexander Hamilton, whose fertile imagination
devised the national debt and envisioned Paterson as a great
manufacturing center. Nobody wins. "The church spires still spend
their wits against the sky." "The rock-table is scratched by the
picnickers' boot-nails, more than by the glacier." The great indus-

trialists are "those guilty bastards . . . trying to undermine us."
The legislators are "under the garbage, uninstructed, incapable of
self-instruction." "An orchestral dulness overlays their world."
"The language, tongue-tied . . . words without style!"

This is the harsh view. Against it is the humorous, the dogs, the
children; lovely fragments of natural description; the author's
sense of the human and sympathetic in his people. Williams is
noted as an imagist, a photographic eye; in Book I he has written
"no ideas but in the facts." This is misleading. His symbolic man
and woman are Hegel's *thesis* and *antithesis*. They struggle toward
synthesis—marriage. But fulness, if it exists at all, only exists in
simple things, trees and animals; so Williams, like other Platonists,
is thrown back on the "idea." "And no whiteness (lost) is so white
as the memory of whiteness." "The stone lives, the flesh dies."
The idea, Beauty, must be realized by the poet where he lives, in
Paterson. "Be reconciled, Poet, with your world, it is the only
truth," though "love" for it "is no comforter, rather a nail in the
skull." *Paterson* is an attempt to write the American Poem. It
depends on the American myth, a myth that is seldom absent from
our literature—part of our power, and part of our hubris and deformity. At its grossest the myth is propaganda, puffing and
grimacing: Size, Strength, Vitality, the Common Man, the New
World, Vital Speech, the Machine; the hideous neo-Roman personae: Democracy, Freedom, Liberty, the Corn, the Land. How
hollow, windy, and inert this would have seemed to an imaginative
man of another culture! But the myth is a serious matter. It is
assumed by Emerson, Whitman, and Hart Crane; by Henry
Adams and Henry James. For good or for evil, America *is* something immense, crass, and Roman. We must unavoidably place
ourselves in our geography, history, civilization, institutions, and
future.

The subjects of great poetry have usually been characters and
the passions, a moral struggle that calls a man's whole person into
play. One thinks of the wrath of Achilles, Macbeth and his conscience, Aeneas debating whether he will leave Dido, whether he
will kill Turnus. But in the best long American poems—*Leaves of
Grass, The Cantos, The Waste Land, Four Quartets, The Bridge,*
and *Paterson*—no characters take on sufficient form to arrive at a
crisis. The people melt into voices. In a recent essay Eliot has
given his reasons why a writer should, perhaps, read Milton;
Williams has answered with an essay that gives reasons why a
writer should *not* read Milton—Eliot and Williams might learn
something from *Paradise Lost* and *Samson Agonistes,* how Milton

populated his desert. Until Books III and IV are published, it is safer to compare *Paterson* with poems that resemble it; not with *The Bridge*, that wonderful monster, so unequal, so inexperienced —dazzling in its rhetoric at times in the way that Keats is dazzling; but with a book in which its admirers profess to find everything, *Leaves of Grass*.

Whitman is a considerable poet, and a considerable myth. I can never quite disentangle the one from the other. I would say that Whitman's language has less variety, sureness and nerve than Williams'; that his imagination is relatively soft, formless, monotonous, and vague. Both poets are strong on compassion and enthusiasm, but these qualities in Whitman are *simpliste* and blurred. *Paterson* is Whitman's America, grown pathetic and tragic, brutalized by inequality, disorganized by industrial chaos, and faced with annihilation. No poet has written of it with such a combination of brilliance, sympathy, and experience, with such alertness and energy. Because he has tried to understand rather than excoriate, and because in his maturity he has been occupied with the "raw" and the universal, his *Paterson* is not the tragedy of the outcast but the tragedy of our civilization. It is a book in which the best readers, as well as the simple reader, are likely to find *everything*.

Charles Olson

Paterson (Book Five)

I didn't find the poem easy just where the poet would seem to have put the weight: the passage of the Cloisters' tapestry on the hunt of the Unicorn.

One is on familiar ground in the other long passage of the poem: "There is a woman in our town," etc., an open man-Sappho poem to a stranger woman seen quickly, and once, on the city street.

There is no distance in the Cloisters passage, such as there was

From *Evergreen Review,* III (Summer 1959), 220-21. Reprinted by permission of the author's estate.

in *Paterson* generally and in this instance here, of the woman. I
liked that distance. It defined the edge of anything, as well as Dr.
Williams' own edge, as he was the 'poet' of 'Paterson.' Here, he is
Paterson him-it self, he is up against the face as closely as the
Cloisters story. It was a point of the old poem, that the poet was
in it to seek a language to deliver men & women from the lump
their lives were without it. The poet was the one to survive the
river and lay the meaning beside its water. My difficulty with the
new poem was that the tapestry, even if the poet called it 'the
living fiction,' was a tapestry—a sewn cloth of flowers, a white
one-horned beast, and the dogs which hunt it. It was not hard to
enjoy the story, or the poem itself as a poem of mottoes written
from it: of the identity of virgin and whore, of the married man
carrying a two-in-one image in his head—the virgin whom he has
whored, of the beast itself wounded, and lay down to rest. It was
the zero distance of the cloth.

I left it to itself, and to Williams, when there it was. Walked by
syllables, flowerword to flowerword the intention of the poet and
the one thing life (or it is actually death) he seems to be saying
has taught him, is what one finds out he has made you do. It is no
longer a matter of a thing. It is a track, a movement after the
collision, which he lays down—and you yield to the step of it from
nothing outside it, including yourself & himself, and take nothing
from it but itself, away.

There is an objectivity (which is there not other than anti-
matter) which forces you, by an unexampled subjectivity of (whom
Williams calls) "I, Paterson, the Kingself" to bring you to his line.

This is what he is talking about, in caps, in the poem when he
says a world of art alone is what has survived since he was young;
and that the only thing which escaped from the hole of death is
'the imagination,' which cannot be fathomed, it is through this
hole we escape, through this hole the imagination escapes intact.
What looks like culture-talk, and that thinking the Doctor so
long has said was not where it was, Not in ideas etc. (NOT
prophecy, he exclaims here), isn't—by the experience of the text
of the poem, in what would appear to be its fussiest, or cutest
(flowers & all that, and at the feet of the beloved) and least
replica passage. Actually and solely, & quite exactly, the poem
offers nothing but *the path* of itself. "Nothing else is real."

I append these passages which shook out then with that meaning:

Paterson VI, he adds: "Words are the burden of poems, poems are made of / words" (P, 281). His belief in the importance of words led to a life long conviction that they should not be prostituted by being turned into complex structures encumbered by levels of symbolic, allusive, or allegorical bric-a-brac and layers of associative resonances. Instead, he viewed the word as a potential "tool," as a structur*ing* rather than a structur*al* unit to be used in the *imitation* rather than the representation of nature. Citing Aristotle's *Poetics* as his source, he defines this imitation in terms of active invention: "To imitate nature involves the verb to do. To copy is merely to reflect something already there, inertly: Shakespeare's mirror is all that is needed for it. But by imitation we enlarge nature itself, we become nature or we discover in ourselves nature's active part" (A, 241). In his Introduction to *William Carlos Williams: A Collection of Critical Essays*, J. Hillis Miller discovers this very process operative in Williams' "Young Sycamore": "Now it is possible to see why Williams makes verbs and verb forms the axis of 'Young Sycamore.' The poem is not a picture of the tree. It is an object which has the same kind of life as the tree. It is an extension of Nature's process. In order to be such an object it must have 'an intrinsic movement of its own to verify its authenticity' " (CCE, 18).

As structuring agents, Williams regarded words in the same light as the materials with which other artists worked, like clay or glass or paint. "Pollock's blobs of paint," he exclaims, "squeezed out / with design! / pure from the tube. Nothing else / is real" (P, 248-249). Aware, however, that words did not come to the poet in a claylike or paintlike state of purity, Williams set out to purify them, to return them, as it were, to an uncorrupted, semantically "prelapsarian" state. It was precisely such an act of purification he felt he detected in the poetry of Marianne Moore: "Miss Moore gets great pleasure from wiping soiled words or cutting them clean out, removing the aureoles that have been pasted about them or taking them bodily from greasy contexts. For the compositions which Miss Moore intends, each word should first stand crystal clear with no attachments; not even an aroma . . . . With Miss Moore a word is a word most when it is separated out by science, treated with acid to remove the smudges, washed, dried and placed right side up on a clean surface" (SE, 128). Williams felt that this purification or "de-smudging" of words involved their being stripped of their artifactual and associative resonances until they were left with only their simplest referential

powers. As Miller describes it, "The word is given reality by the
fact it names, but the independence of the fact from the word
frees the word to be a fact in its own right and at the same time
'dynamizes' it with meaning" (CCE, 11).

To gain a clearer understanding of both the nature and implica-
tions of Williams' attitude toward the role of words in his poetry
it will prove helpful to examine briefly Claude Levi-Strauss'
definition, in *The Savage Mind* (1962), of the artist as part engineer and part *bricoleur*. The word *"bricoleur"* presents some difficulty in that there is no precise English equivalent for it. It
transliterates as "handyman" or "jack-of-all-trades" but, as Levi-
Strauss explains, it carries the additional connotation of using
"devious means compared to those of a craftsman" (SM, 16-17).
The *bricoleur* uses materials which were designed for another
purpose, materials described by Gérard Genette in "Structuralisme
et Critique Litteraire" (1965) as the "residue of human artifacts."
Levi-Strauss opposes the model of the *bricoleur* to that of the
engineer and differentiates between the two as follows:

> The bricoleur is adept at performing a large number of diverse
> tasks; but, unlike the engineer, he does not subordinate each of
> them to the availability of raw materials and tools conceived
> and procured for the purpose of the project. His universe of in-
> struments is closed and the rules of his game are always to make
> do with 'whatever is at hand,' that is to say with a set of tools
> and materials which is always finite and is also heterogeneous
> because what it contains bears no relation to the current project,
> or indeed to any particular project, but is the contingent result of
> all the occasions there have been to renew or enrich the stock
> or to maintain it with the remains of previous constructions or
> destructions. (SM, 17)

The engineer, on the other hand, uses "as many sets of tools and
materials or 'instrumental sets,' as there are different kinds of
projects" (SM, 17).

Since the *bricoleur*, who is likened by Levi-Strauss to the myth-
maker, works with a finite and residual set of materials and the
engineer constantly creates new instrumental sets to accommodate
the particular project, "the engineer is always trying to make his
way out of and go beyond the constraints imposed by a particular
state of civilization while the *bricoleur* by inclination or necessity
always remains within them" (SM, 19). We may infer from Levi-
Strauss' definitions that the *bricoleur* defines his "tools" or "mate-

rials" strictly in terms of the particular project whereas the engineer tends to define his project functionally in terms of the instrumental sets or tools he creates for its execution. The former is a defining of means (structur*al* units) in terms of ends (the particular project) whereas the latter is a defining of ends (the particular project) in terms of the means (functioning, hence structur*ing* agents). We may also infer that the artist—in Levi-Strauss' sense of him as part engineer and part *bricoleur*—moves closer to the *bricoleur* to the degree that he accepts and utilizes a language and a poetics which are heavily artifactual and residual, or, more kindly, *tradition-conscious* and derivative, and moves closer to the engineer to the degree that he attempts to create new techniques and a new vocabulary to serve his formal designs. The former defines his poetic self in terms of the particular choices he makes and the particular traditions in which he invests, whereas the latter defines himself most precisely in terms of the innovative avenues through which he tries to approach new modes of poetry.

An excellent—if rather predictable—example of the poet-as-*bricoleur* would be T. S. Eliot, who consciously placed himself in the mainstream of "poetic tradition" and invested almost every word of his poetry with what I have called "artifactual" resonances, i.e., allusion, symbolism, allegory—all of those poetic techniques which force a poem into participation synchronically and diachronically with the rest of literature and culture. On the other hand, it would be difficult to imagine a poet who so nearly approaches the role of poet-as-engineer as Williams (which, as we shall see, accounts for no small part of Williams' antipathy for Eliot and the "academics"). Williams, for example, would not, in all probability, have said "new modes of poetry." More likely he would have said something like "new ways of making poems." And there were two primary drives—it would not be far wrong to call them obsessions—which underlay virtually every aspect of his poem-making. The first, which we have already lightly touched on, was his insistence upon purifying or "combing out" (P, 173) the language. The second was his compulsion to marry art and life, most often expressed obversely as his refusal to condone their separation. These axiomatic poetic principles and the thematic and structural consequences they obtain in *Paterson* are germane to any reading of the poem, and a clearer understanding of them should make accessible much that has heretofore seemed opaque or merely chaotic to its readers.

Williams' purification of language is alternately imagined in *Paterson* as a kind of purging by fire and as a kind of breaking down or "chemical" reduction of the word, divesting it of the clutter of associative meanings (or smudges) which have accrued to it. In the former case the poet imagines himself as a kind of Vulcan, transmuting words in much the same way as the fire acts upon the glass bottle in Book III: "An old bottle, mauled by the fire / gets a new glaze, the glass warped / to a new distinction, reclaiming the / undefined" (P, 142—143). Clearly the passage evokes a sense of the poet as a reclaimer of the inherent beauty possessed originally by the natural "thing." Accordingly, the poet seems here to have hit upon a way to unlock the beauty which, he originally complained, was "locked in the mind past all remonstrance" (P, 11). Reclaiming, in this sense, seems to mean something very close to unlocking. But we find, as the poet continues to contemplate the bottle, that more of an active and inventive role is imagined for the poet than simply that of reclaimer: "The glass / splotched with concentric rainbows / of cold fire that the fire has bequeathed / there as it cools, its flame / defied—the flame that wrapped the glass / deflowered, reflowered there by / the flame: a second flame, surpassing / heat" (P, 143). Like the fire the poet must bequeath as well as reclaim or unlock; not only must he "warp" (as in the first passage)—he must also "wrap." The parallel seems to have been very striking to Williams; he returns to it a third time: "Poet Beats Fire at Its Own Game! The bottle! / the bottle! the bottle! the bottle! I / give you the bottle!" (P, 143).

But there is a cautionary note. Though the poet must work like Vulcan upon his material, upon language, he must be careful to imitate nature here as elsewhere; the fire, in other words, must only be a catalyst to the natural forces of diachrony: "Here's a fossil conch (a paper weight / of sufficient quaintness) mud / and shells baked by a near eternity / into a melange, hard as stone, full of / tiny shells / —baked by endless dessications into / a shelly rime;" (P, 170). Incautious imitation or interruption of natural forces is catastrophic to art, ruining it like the 400-grain pearl is ruined by its shell being boiled open (P, 17).

The second kind of purification of language—the divesting of the word of its smudges—is delineated in *Paterson* by the recurrent images of "divorce" and "breakup" which signify knowledge. The old forms must be destroyed in order to release the new ones: "—to dissect away / the block and leave / a separate metal" (P, 207). These themes—of divorce, breakup, reduction—are opposed to the recurrent motif of blockage or non-communication which finds its central signification in the figure of the library where

"texts mount and complicate them- / selves, lead to further texts
and those / to synopses, digests and emendations. So be it" (P,
156). Hence, *dissolution*, which Levi-Strauss posits as the ultimate
goal of science (SM, 247), rather than *constitution* leads to discovery and, as such, is what deserves credit: "Uranium: basic
thought—leadward / Fractured: radium: credit" (P, 217). It is
by this ongoing process of recognizing dissonance, forcing dissolution, and gaining discovery that the poet remakes his world just
as the engineer remakes his; by clearing blockage and dissolving
complex residual or artifactual structures both the poet and engineer transcend the "constraints imposed by a particular state of
civilization" (SM, 19).

It is necessary here to deal with what seems to be an inner
contradiction in Williams' poetic strategies as I have described
them. Is there not a fundamental contradiction between the idea
of working in congruence with the natural forces of diachrony on
the one hand and the idea of "recognizing dissonance, forcing
dissolution, and thereby gaining discovery" as deserving of credit
on the other? The answer lies in recognizing, as Williams unmistakably did, that insofar as language goes the poet lives in a fallen
and corrupted world. Before the poet can catalyze or "touch with
fire" the central energies of nature—assimilated, as they are, into
his poetic imagination—he must first dissolve the complex structures which have grown about words. Once these artifactual
smudges have been removed, he is ready to use the word, "not to
smear it again with thinking (the attachments of thought) but in
such a way that it will remain scrupulously itself, clean perfect,
unnicked beside other words in parade" (SE, 128—129). And, I
should reiterate, for Williams the imitation of nature—here imagined as remaining faithful to her diachronic workings—in no way
connoted the representation of its energies; instead it explicitly
connoted the assimilation of those energies into a poetic consciousness dedicated to the extension or *remaking* of nature. It is precisely this assimilation of nature's central energies which attains,
in Williams' poetry, the decidedly linear and temporal thrust (as
opposed to spatial) which Miller and others have noted. One of
Williams' poems is, in other words, the precipitate, the visible
result of the poet's remaking of self and world through the intro-
version and catalysis of nature's central energies *in a purified
language.*

Williams' insistence upon the co-incidence of natural and artistic
energies is manifest in his refusal to separate art space and life

space. Here again like the engineer who relates the enclosed and non-referential world of mathematics to the plastic physical world, the poet, according to Williams, must intimately relate his experience to his poetry and vice versa, otherwise both are worthless: "You might as well take all your own literature and everyone else's and toss it into one of those big garbage trucks of the Sanitation Department, so long as the people with the top-cream minds and the 'finer' sensibilities use those minds and sensibilities not to make themselves more humane human beings than the average person, but merely as means of ducking responsibility toward a better understanding of their fellow man, except theoretically—which doesn't mean a God dammed thing" (P, 101). Following the visual arts here as elsewhere, Williams sought to imitate the cubists' synthesis of life space and art space as Jerome Mazzaro describes in "Dimensionality in Dr. Williams' *Paterson*" (1970): "But as it was the problem of dimensionality which finally forced the cubists to invent the collage, it is the problem of dimensionality which finally forces Williams into the innovations of *Paterson*, for it is not until Williams begins to incorporate items from newspapers and segments of historical documents and letters that one can say that art space begins to intrude on life space and the collage begins." Ralph Nash in "The Use of Prose in *Paterson*" (1953), an article which drew a very enthusiastic response from Williams, also describes how the inclusion of prose blocks into *Paterson* affects the prosody and effects a marriage of life space and art space.

But Williams seemed to be looking for more than just a marriage of these two spaces; he seemed to be seeking a coincidental space, some primal meeting ground where the "actual" and the "imaginative" existed simultaneously. Williams often imagined the task in terms of destroying the distance between self and world, between life-subject and art-object. He seems to be describing an experience wherein he achieved this fusion in "The Wanderer": "Then the river began to enter my heart . . . / Till I felt the very depth of its rottenness . . . / And dropped down knowing this was me now . . . It tortured itself within me / Until time had been washed finally under . . . / And I knew all—it became me" (CEP, 11—12). This vision of inner-other synthesis is not so much an attempt to negate the ego—as Miller is led to conclude in *Poets of Reality* (1965) by such lines as "Why speak of I which interests me almost not at all" (P, 30)—as it is a vision of the relationship between self and other as one of intensive intervolve-ment or interpenetration which is at once real and aestheticized. It involves a more active participation of the ego than, for example, Merleau-Ponty ascribes to it in his image of the ego as the darkness in the theater which makes visible the image on the screen; such a submissive or self-negating role for the ego would pre-empt all of Williams' notions of the artist assimilating nature's energies and extending them in his transformation of his materials. Like Keats's idea of negative capability—and it is worth noting that Keats was Williams' first poetic model—the vision seemed to involve a precarious balance between, on the one hand, the stamping of the poet's identity upon the artistic materials and, on the other, the willingness to enslave the poetic self to the overwhelming reality of the "other" in a capitulation of ontogenetic potential to phylogenetic momentum. The first alternative would lead to sentimentalism, moralism, or anthropomorphism of one variety or another, while the second would lead to a "Shakespeare's mirror" type of representation which Williams rejected.

Williams incarnates his primal space wherein art and life are one in the "beautiful thing" of Books III and IV. The "beautiful thing" first appeared in *Paterson: Episode 17* (CEP, 438—442) in the form of a young Negress beating a rug but, significantly, in *Paterson III* and *IV* the form remains ambiguous and mutable. At first he imagines the beautiful thing as a counter-symbol to the library: "a roar of books / from the wadded library oppresses him / until / his mind begins to drift. / Beautiful thing: / —a dark flame, / a wind, a flood—counter to all staleness" (P, 123). Again he opposes the blockage of the library to the counter-staleness of the beautiful thing: "The Library is desolation, it has a smell of its own / of stagnation and death. / Beautiful Thing!" (P, 123). In the ensuing burning of the library (which finally destroys the city but lights the night) the beautiful thing comes to be associated with the defiance of authority ("Beautiful thing! aflame. / a defiance of authority" [P, 144]), with the fire itself ("Beautiful thing / —intertwined with the fire. An identity / surmounting the world, its core—from which / we shrink squirting little hoses of / objection" [P, 145]), and finally with the "Poet" (P, 145). Shortly thereafter the beautiful thing is described as simultaneously ideal and real, imaginative and actual; it is, at one time, the entelechy of forms and the "flame's lover," art and life: "Beautiful Thing! / Let them explain you and you will be / the heart of the explanation. Nameless. / you will appear / Beautiful Thing / the flame's lover—" (P, 148). Finally the poet is "shaken by your beauty. / Shaken" (P, 148). Williams selects this moment to introduce the figure of the unicorn which dominates Book V: "A tapestry hound / with his thread teeth drawing crimson from / the throat of the unicorn" (P, 152) and it is apparent that some kind of equation is being drawn between the rending of the unicorn by the hound and the maltreatment of the beautiful thing which both precedes it ("You showed me your legs, scarred (as a child) / by the whip" [P, 152]) and follows it ("the guys from Paterson . . . socked you one / across the nose / Beautiful Thing / for good luck and emphasis / cracking it" [P, 153]). As we shall see, there is an excellent reason for Williams' introduction of the unicorn symbol into the poem precisely at this point; first, however, we must understand what motivated Williams to turn to the medieval tapestries of The Cloisters and, in doing so, to a poetic interest in the past which, at first sight, seems to run counter to his lifelong rejection of poetic traditionality and historical "residue."

In his *Autobiography* (1948) Williams succinctly describes his well-known hostility for T. S. Eliot's poetry: "These were the years just before the great catastrophe to our letters—the appearance of T. S. Eliot's *The Waste Land*. There was heat in us, a core and drive that was gathering headway upon the theme of a rediscovery of a primary impetus, the elementary principle of all art, in the local conditions. Our work staggered to a halt for a moment under the blast of Eliot's genius which gave the poem back to the academics. We did not know how to answer him" (A, 146). I have already, at the risk of oversimplification, characterized Eliot as a poet-as-*bricoleur* who chose to derive much of his poetics from the 17th-century metaphysical tradition. Here again, Williams' response to Eliot is unequivocal: "Let the metaphysical take care of itself," he writes, "the arts have nothing to do with it. They will concern themselves with it if they please, among other things" (SE, 256). Unlike Eliot, who forced his poems into participation with the body of literature and cultural historicity, Williams sought a return to nature through imitation. By purifying language, by shunning traditional techniques of "drasty rymying" (P, 208) and strict schemes of meter and footage in favor of the variable foot "consistent with a relativistic age" Williams fought the oppression of the past with aesthetic innovation.

Yet suddenly, in *Paterson V*, Williams turns to an art tradition rooted in the past. As Walter Sutton writes in "Dr. Williams' *Paterson* and the Quest for Form": "There is also a greater concern for the past in *Paterson V*, not, as in the earlier books, in terms of its destructive and inhibiting influences, but rather as a source of tradition in art that has sustained and guided the modern artist." There seem to be two reasons for Williams breaking away from his former conviction that "past objects have about them past necessities—like the sonnet—which have conditioned them and from which, as a form itself, they cannot be freed" (A, 265). First, Williams seems to have been trying—whether consciously or not—to find a sustaining tradition for art which would specifically exclude the tradition defined by Eliot: most of the artists named in *Paterson V* predate Donne (Shakespeare, Dante, da Vinci, Bosch, Peter Brueghel the Elder, Sappho). Second, in the dominant symbol "the unicorn against a millefleurs background" (P, 268), Williams found the perfect artistic example of the marriage of the actual and the imaginative, the scientific and the mythic, the real and the ideal, art and life; in short, his "beautiful thing."

The unicorn had long been used by artists as a symbol for what Carl Jung, in *Psychology and Alchemy* (1953), terms "the paradoxical nature of the unconscious . . . thought of either as the *materia* itself or as its essence or *anima*, which was designated with the name 'Mercurius.' " Being double-natured the unicorn could signify either good or evil. It could, for example, signify Christ tamed in the lap of the virgin like Jehovah (terrible beyond measure) tamed by the Virgin Mary into the God of Love of the New Testament (PA, 424). On the other hand it could signify rampant sexual energy. For Williams it maintained this ambivalence and alternately signifies the sexual energy which pervades *Paterson V:* "The Unicorn roams the forest of all true / lovers' minds. They hunt it down. Bow wow! sing hey the / green holly!" (P, 272) and what Thomas R. Whitaker describes in *Williams Carlos Williams* (1968) as the "King-self, the imagination without peer" (WCW, 148). Whether envisioned as aggressive sexual energy or as sublimated 'creative' energy, Williams felt that the energy must be voluntarily controlled or imprisoned within the realm of the actual or real. This is evidenced both by his characteristic sexual fantasizing (e.g., the woman of the town who "walks rapidly, flat bellied / in worn slacks upon the street" [P, 255]) and by his categorical rejection of all those artistic strategies he considered outmoded or inconsistent with an age of relativism. The picture of the imprisoned unicorn served as a perfect figure or emblem for Williams since it depicts the unicorn (mythos, sexuality, imagination) "penned by a low / wooden fence" (P, 270) (indicating either that the imprisonment is voluntary or that the strength of the unicorn is waning) in a field of flowers depicted with such realistic detail that over sixty species have been identified by botanists. Herein Williams felt he had found an art tradition rooted in the past which also insisted upon marrying the real and the imaginative, the mythic and the scientific. And, although it may have been only fortuitous, it is interesting that the tradition he selected evolved from a medieval epistemology based on *cognition* rather than *perception*, a theory of human understanding which presumes no separation between subject and object.

Paterson V can be read along the lines suggested by Whitaker, as a marriage of the "King-self, the imagination without peer" to the "virgin-whore in all her phases" (WCW, 148). Or it can be read with the same mixture of sympathy and humor with which Williams regarded himself as a portrait of the aging poet saddened and amused by his own dwindling sexual and artistic potency: "Paterson has grown older / the dog of his thoughts / has shrunk / to no more than 'a passionate letter' / to a woman, a woman he had neglected / to put to bed in the past. / And went on / living and writing / answering / letters / and tending his flower / garden" (P, 268). In either case the picture of the unicorn against the millefleurs background serves as a viable emblem of the poetic self, the poet-as-engineer involved in the struggle to intervolve the *mythos* of self with the *eidos* of nature.

Finally, on the level of formal design Williams was also a kind of practicing engineer. That he was concerned with attaining a sense of form is unquestionable; toward the end of Book III he writes: "How to begin to find a shape—to begin to begin again . . . seems beyond attainment" (P, 167). Here again, however, as on the level of the tool, on the level of the project one must always look for the ongoing or dynamic process. As Walter Sutton writes:

> Through his measured expression the poet achieves the only reality he can ever know. This reality, figured as a dance, is dynamic and relative rather than static and absolute. The poet of *Paterson* concludes, or at least interrupts himself, on this note:
>
> > We know nothing and can know nothing
> >   but
> > the dance, to dance to a measure
> > contrapuntally,
> >
> >   Satyrically, the tragic foot.   (P, 278)
>
> The dance, at any given time and place, is also a form which is tentative, straining toward completion, subject to change. In short, a dynamic, organic form.

But whereas Williams' conception of reality as something "dynamic and relative" led him, on the level of technique and style, to the variable foot, a linear and temporal thrust, and a purified language, on the level of formal design it seems to have led him to what Levi-Strauss calls the *constitutive dialectic* as opposed to the *dissolving process of analysis* (the latter of which, as we have seen, so typifies Williams' attitude toward language). Opposing Jean-Paul Sartre's view, Levi-Strauss defines the constitutive dialective as "the bridge, forever extended and improved, which analytical reason throws out over an abyss; it is unable to see the further shore but it knows that it is there, even should it be constantly receding" (SM, 246). Dialectical reason, for Levi-Strauss, is analytical reason "roused to action, tensed by its efforts to transcend itself" (SM, 246). It seems, then, that the same impulse which led Williams to a purgational reductionism on the semantic level led him to a self-transcending constructionism on the level of form and vision. It is almost impossible to read Levi-Strauss' description of dialectical reason as "the bridge, forever extended and improved" being projected (in both senses of the word) over the abyss toward an invisible (and possibly receding) shore without thinking of Williams spinning out the poem *Paterson* like one of his tightrope walkers—De Lave, Harry Leslie, George Dobbs— adding book after book and leaving fragments toward an uncompleted book. This commitment to a vision of "becoming" in the Bergsonian sense was always present in Williams' poetry. It was there in the young sycamore, in the happy genius of the household, in the image of the mind imagined as "a red stone carved to be / endless flight" (P, 63). It was there in the beautiful thing in all its forms and in the unicorn against the millefleurs background. It is finally and most uncompromisingly there in the form of *Paterson V* itself which, by its very existence, refutes (or transcends) the conclusion to *Paterson IV:*

> This is the blast
> the eternal close
> the spiral
> the final somersault
> the end.

As a purifier of language Williams may have been trying to get back to the beginnings, but as a dialectician he assured readers there would be no end.

Jerome Mazzaro

Dimensionality in Dr. Williams' *Paterson*

If the poetry of William Carlos Williams was to pass through a kind of cubism in the twenties and thirties, it is out of this cubism that the structure of his long poem *Paterson* emerges. As Wylie Sypher indicates in *Rococo to Cubism in Art and Literature* (1960), cubism has its equivalent in the relativism of F. H. Bradley, Albert Einstein, and Alfred North Whitehead: "The cubist world is the world of a new physics," of a reality "that . . . can have no absolute contours but varies with the angle from which one sees it." Its various perspectives as they reflect the plurality of identities common to Pragmatism define the identity of things as the views one takes of them, or as Whitehead later called it, one's "prehensions" of them. Yet, as Clement Greenberg remarks in *Art and Culture* (1961), the very alteration in the composition of an art work which cubism produces leads to serious new problems regarding perspective: "By that time, flatness had not only invaded but was threatening to swamp the Cubist picture. The little facet-planes into which Braque and Picasso were dissecting everything visible now all lay parallel to the picture plane. They were no longer controlled, either in drawing or in placing, by linear or even scalar perspective. Each facet tended to be shaded, moreover, as an independent unit, with no legato passages, no unbroken tracts of value gradation on its open side, to join it to adjacent facet-planes." "The main problem at this juncture," he goes on to note, "became to keep the 'inside' of the picture—its content—from fusing with the 'outside'—its literal surface. *Depicted* flatness—that is, the facet-planes—had to be kept separate enough from *literal* flatness to permit a minimal illusion of three-dimensional space to survive between the two."

As a way out of this problem, Braque and Picasso jointly hit upon the notion of the collage where, as Greenberg records, "the illusion of depth created by the contrast between the affixed material and everything else gives way immediately to an illusion of forms in bas-relief, which gives way in turn, with equal imme-

From *Modern Poetry Studies*, I (1970), 98-117. Reprinted by permission of the journal.

diacy, to an illusion that seems to contain both—or neither." This collage technique which art historians grant as a major turning point in the evolution both of cubism and of modernist art marks the shift from analytical to synthetic cubism, though, as Greenberg insists, synthetic cubism did not fully begin there. He places its beginning when Picasso carried "the forward push of the collage (and of Cubism in general) *literally* into the literal space in front of the picture plane." Picasso did this by cutting and folding a piece of paper in the shape of a guitar and gluing and fitting to it four taut strings and other pieces of paper. He created thereby a sequence of "flat surfaces in real and sculptured space to which there clung only the vestige of a picture plane." This new dimensionality while in no way returning to the fixed point of perspective proves the cubist's ability to assimilate into his pictorial world at the precise point where art and life intersect elements of actuality previously alien to painting. He has, in short, moved art space into life space. It remained for the Spanish painter, Juan Gris, to carry on the technique of the collage after it had been abandoned by its inventors.

Moreover, if the image of this relative universe would cause conflicts in the arrangements of perspective in art, it would also cause certain conflicts in a poet whose *Kora in Hell* (1920) asserted that poetry was a cycle of descent and return where "at the sickening turn toward death the pieces are joined into a pretty thing . . . art . . . a thing to carry up with you on the next turn." He, too, as he moved toward cubism would need something as drastic as the collage if his art were to lose the flatness inherent there. In *Spring and All* (1923), he gives over a section of the work to a discussion of Gris's techniques. He particularly praises his practice of using real objects *literally* in his collages: "Here is a shutter, a bunch of grapes, a sheet of music, a picture of sea and mountains (particularly fine) which the onlooker is not for a moment permitted to witness as an 'illusion.'" As Daniel-Henry Kahnweiler asserts in *Juan Gris, His Life His Work* (1969), "Even in the early days, in 1912, he used pages from books and pieces of mirror in his pictures; but whereas, with Picasso in particular, the newspaper was often used simply as a piece of material, with Gris the fragment of mirror represents a mirror, the printed book page is itself, and so is the piece of newspaper . . . . 'You want to know why I had to stick on a piece of mirror?' he said to [Michel] Leiris. 'Well, surfaces can be re-created and volumes interpreted in a picture, but what is one to do about a mirror whose surface is always changing and which should reflect even the spectator? There is nothing else to do but stick on a real piece.' " Williams repeats the praise in letters to Charles Henri Ford (1930) and Kay Boyle (1932) as well as in his *Autobiography* (1951) and *A Novelette and Other Prose (1921—1931)* (1932). To Ford, he admits, "That man was my perfect artist." To Kay Boyle, he challenges, "Why do we not read more of Juan Gris? He knew these things [how art form is intrinsic in the times] in painting and wrote well of them." This last is most likely an allusion to Gris's "Des Possibilités de la Peinture" (1924), the last part of which appeared in the *Transatlantic Review* in an issue containing the Mayflower section of Williams' *In the American Grain* (1925).

Yet the two poems which Williams constructs to accompany his discussion and endorsement of Gris in *Spring and All,* like his earlier cubist poem "To a Solitary Disciple" (1916), in no way affix "real" objects to their surfaces, however much they may realize the effects of Gris's method, described by Williams in prose: "One thing laps over on the other, the cloud laps over the shutter, the bunch of grapes is part of the handle of the guitar, the mountain and sea are obviously not 'the mountain and sea,' but a picture of the mountain and the sea. All drawn with admirable simplicity and excellent design—all a unity." Williams' first poem, entitled "The Rose" in *The Collected Earlier Poems* (1951), describes the "fragility of the flower / unbruised" which "penetrates space," but the poem itself does not penetrate space by similarly affixing the shape of a literal flower to its surface. Likewise, in approximating cubist displacement, "At the Faucet of June" makes no advance toward synthetic cubism. While more like Braque, "The Dish of Fruit" (1945) in *The Collected Later Poems* in no way furthers the poem as cubist experience. A description of an object is not the process of its multilevel perception; the cubist subject matter of these poems simply does not make them cubist in execution.

If one were to consider two kinds of prose or two kinds of poetry or prose and poetry as two different facet-planes because of different moods or different densities, one might argue that the text and commentary of *Kora,* which vacillates between roman and italic type, or "The Testament of Perpetual Change" (1948), which carries on the same vacillation in poetry, or the text and prose of *Spring and All* might be considered cubist, albeit they would at best make a kind of analytical rather than synthetic cubism. This seems to be the position of Williams, who in a chapter of *A Novelette* entitled "Juan Gris" remarks: "[Ezra] Pound will say that the improvisations [that is, *Kora in Hell*] are . . . twenty, forty years late. On the contrary . . . their excellence is, in major part, the shifting of category. It is the disjointing process." Still, that would make a work like Dante's *La Vita Nuova*, based upon a similar mixture of prose and poetry, a proto-cubist work as would be Giordano Bruno's *Heroic Frenzies* and Petronius' *Satyricon*. And if John C. Thirlwall is correct in "William Carlos Williams' *Paterson*" (1961) in spotting Williams' ultimate indebtedness not to Chaucer's *Canterbury Tales* but to an early reading of *Aucassin and Nicolette*, this work becomes proto-cubist as well. Georges Lemaitre is willing to entertain such notions in painting in *From Cubism to Surrealism in French Literature* (1947) when he makes cubist art relatable to medieval multiple depictions of saints' lives.

Yet there is another element of cubism, its reduction of shapes to geometric forms which must also be considered. One cannot dismiss Paul Cézanne's oft-quoted statement, "Represent nature by means of the cylinder, the sphere, the cone," or the cubist's tendency to "destroy" objects by reshaping them into intelligent "pictorial facts." Here one might find the equation of a work of literature with cubist art hardest to hold, although one might argue that Williams' reduction of thoughts to their nonsentimental expressions may be a suitable verbal equivalent to the reduction of objects to their geometric shapes. Nevertheless, the point is that, however impossible it may be that cubist art can be translated into cubist poetry, Williams clearly conceived of the problems of dimensionality in poetry to be similar to the problems of dimensionality in cubism and sought, however wrong-headedly, to solve these problems in poetic equivalents to paint. Nor was Williams alone in his belief of the interrelatedness of poetry and cubism. There was Guillaume Apollinaire and, as Kahnweiler points out, Gris in the *Open Windows* series, used by Williams for his example in *Spring and All*, was himself trying to translate painting into "poetry."

For Apollinaire, who abandons traditional punctuation and emphasizes the obscure, the disjointed, and the jerky in the verses of *Alcools* (1913), a mystical element lay in the dissolving surfaces and attempts to seize "l'univers infini comme idéal." The element is not common to Williams nor to Gris, but it informs the work of poets like E. E. Cummings, Archibald MacLeish, and Kenneth

Rexroth as well as affords the basis of what is normally considered "cubist poetry." Gris's own "poetry" was another matter. Kahnweiler describes it as "signs" which Gris used as "emblems": "They *are* a knife or a glass. They are never symbols, for they never have a dual identity . . . . They *are* the objects which they represent, with all the emotive values attaching to them; but they never signify anything outside of these objects." By their repetition in one or a sequence of paintings these signs become "rhymes" which "reveal to the beholder certain hidden relationships, similarities between two apparently different objects." "In 1920," Kahnweiler notes, "these metaphors are fairly evident and are based on the simplest objects (playing card, glasses etc.). Then a bunch of grapes is compared to a mandolin (1921). Finally, objects of increasingly disparate character are reconciled through more inventive 'rhymes.' In the *Portrait of a Woman* of 1922, for example, the woman's head is repeated in her hand. In *The Nun of* 1922, the whole figure is repeated in reverse in the clasped hands and the folds of the sleeves. In *Three Masks* of 1923, the rhymes have become still more numerous and the head of each figure is repeated in the folds of their garments, their arms, etc."

To complete these "rhymes," Gris altered, but never abandoned Cézanne's famous pronunciamento. As he wrote for *L'Esprit Nouveau* (1921), he wanted to "humanize" art: "Cézanne turns a bottle into a cylinder, but I begin with a cylinder and create an individual of a special type: I make a bottle—a particular bottle—out of a cylinder." In the *Transatlantic Review*, he describes the result in terms of a weaving metaphor: "Painting for me is like a fabric, all of a piece and uniform, with one set of threads as the representational, aesthetic element, and the crossthreads as the technical, architectural, or abstract element. These threads are interdependent and complementary, and if one set is lacking the fabric does not exist." In *A Novelette*, Williams translates this image of warp and woof into the crossthreads of novelistic conversation and novelistic design: "Always the one thing in Juan Gris. Conversation as design. Were it not so—it is less than actual, it is covered, dull, a makeshift. I have always admired and partaken of Juan Gris. Singly he says that the actual is the drawing of the face—and so the face borrowing of the drawing—by lack of copying and lack of a burden to the story—is real."

In "Marianne Moore" (1931), Williams discusses the appearance of this "fabric" in poetry: "The interstices for the light and not the interstitial web of the thought concerned her, or so it seems to me. Thus the material is as the handling: the thought, the word, the rhythm—all in the style. The effect is in the penetration of the light itself, how much, how little; the appearance of the luminous background." Or, as he says in more practical terms, "There are two elements essential to Miss Moore's scheme of composition, the hard and unaffected concept of the apple itself as an idea, then its edge-to-edge contact with the things which surround it . . . . The thought is used exactly as the apple, it is the same insoluble block." In a second essay on Miss Moore, published in 1948, he makes his association of her and the cubists even more explicit: "Miss Moore has taken recourse to the mathematics of art. Picasso does no different: a portrait is a stratagem singularly related to a movement among the means of the craft. By making these operative, relationships become self-apparent."

In this translation, words take on some of the characteristics which pigments in cubist painting took on as it moved toward synthetic cubism and, under Braque and Picasso, began to thicken its paints with sand or ashes. As Kahnweiler notes, "This 'solidification' of the color was intended to diminish the viscous appearance of oil paint and so restrict the possibility of virtuosity in the execution . . . . The painters of 1912 felt that the medium created by painters of the fifteenth century was no longer adequate to their purpose, which was so radically different from the Renaissance." Comparably, having described how for Miss Moore "a word is a word most when it is separated out by science, treated with acid to remove the smudges, washed, dried and placed right side up on a clean surface," Williams goes on to note, "It may be used not to smear it again with thinking (the attachments of thought) but in such a way that it will remain scrupulously itself, clean perfect, unnicked beside other words in parade." This "solidification," which is anticipated in his assertion that "particles of language must be clear as sand" and in his generally "cubist" remarks on Edgar Allan Poe in *In the American Grain*, he makes part of Miss Moore's modernity. It is the reduction of Dante's "illustrious" and consequently fourfold symbolizing language in *De Vulgari Eloquentia* to something more worldly and equates with his even earlier emphasis in Prologue to *Kora* on language's true rather than associational or sentimental value.

But as it was the problem of dimensionality which finally forced the cubists to invent the collage, it is the problem of dimensionality which finally forces Williams into the innovations of *Paterson*, for it is not until Williams begins to incorporate items from newspapers and segments of historical documents and letters that one can say that art space begins to intrude on life space and the collage begins. This intrusion, the reverse of the "background effects" of quotations in Pound's *Cantos* and T. S. Eliot's *The Waste Land*, comes after other experiments with dimensionality, and it is with these that one should perhaps begin. Yet, as with his poems generally, the degree to which the success of these experiments depends upon the effects of Williams' intention and not upon the unconscious elements present will for the moment remain unexplored.

Language, syntax, punctuation, spacing, setting, shifts in voice, tense, mood, and thought, for example, form the traditional shapes of dimensionality in Williams' early poems. The reader accordingly moved from life into and through the art work and returned to life. This process which approximates the Kora myth and the process of poetry described in *Kora in Hell* is apparent in such poems as "A Coronal" (1920). The poem begins with the prediction of fall, of Kora's annual descent into Hell. Although set in a future tense, the prediction is based upon regular recurrence rather than upon a novel event. This occurrence is stated in the passive voice. The very essence of the voice indicates man's inability to alter the season's course. When one does move into the realm of the controlable and the active voice, a "we" intrudes and an abrupt new facet-plane begins. This emergence is accented by the coordinating conjunction "but," which begins the stanza as well as the stanza's shift into a past tense. One shifts again immediately in the next line into a new facet-plane as not only a new person is introduced in the impersonal "one" but a new point in futurity is described. This point is past fall in spring and the return of Kora, suggested now by the use of the personal pronoun "her." Thus a reader is drawn into a dimensionality created by Williams mainly through time-shifts within a sequence of occurrences which brings him from autumn to spring, from expectation to fulfillment. With this fulfillment the reader is released into the life space he enjoyed before he began reading.

"History" realizes this process more graphically as it takes its reader from an outside setting into the interior of a museum and then returns him to the outdoors, again much as Kora is taken into Hell and then returned to earth. This more obvious use of setting in no way diminishes Williams' handling of shifts in time and person to create facet-planes. It does permit him, however, to add to the predominantly time illusion of "A Coronal" an illusion of space by naming a sequence of objects to convey a passage by those objects. Yet it is "To a Solitary Disciple," which, as an early "cubist" work, offers the reader the closest approximation of the problems in dimensionality which Williams had to face. It begins with three disparate concepts kept separate from life by their beginning with "rather" and kept parallel to each other by the repetition of the word. Instead of an invitation toward descent, as the first word of the poem, "rather" immediately cuts the work off from life in a way similar to that in which a frame cuts off an easel picture from life. The poem goes on to pose alternatives which, like the reverse images in the "poetry" of Gris's paintings, conclude in a series of three unqualified commands to observe. The parallelism which begins with the moon's being opposed to the steeple thus ends with the edifice's being opposed to lightness. Yet in this progress a flatness emerges similar to the flatness of a painting, which may well be what Williams intends to describe. Consequently there is no depth and no descent; the reader remains throughout in the platform space of life as if the facet-planes which were being created were fusing into the literal flatness of the page. The final observation of the poem which turns not on life but on the opening observation forces the reader into as abrupt a return to life as had been his entrance into the work. The lesson has been concluded for the disciple by the master's silence. The same flatness occurs in "The Rose" and "The Dish of Fruit."

Only "At the Faucet of June" among these previously mentioned early "cubist" poems offers an exception. It introduces a dimensionality which reverses the carefully controlled inner descent of "History." Its abrupt assertion of a patch of yellow on a varnished floor is followed by a permissive wandering of the mind, descending, so to speak, into facet-planes that depict the realms of memory and imagination. The wandering ends more ethereally than Williams' poems are wont to conclude, suggestive perhaps of the "mystical element" in some kinds of cubism; but the illusion of dimension created by the associational drift through time is clear. Like Kora one can descend through it. "Paterson" (1927), whose "cylindrical trees" and "complex mathematic" suggest even in this early draft that it, too, was intended as a "cubist" poem, moves from spring to a winter described so as to remind the reader of spring's return. Similarly it allows a dimensionality of descent and return; yet the descents of none of these poems constitute a noticeable intrusion of art into life.

This lack of intrusion into life may account for the sense of artistic failure which Williams expresses in a letter to Horace Gregory shortly before he began the work of putting together the final version of *Paterson*. That he felt he had to find a new method for the poem is clear. He mentions the need both to Gregory and to James Laughlin and records the crisis in his *Autobiography*. To Gregory he writes, "The old approach is outdated, and I shall have to work like a fiend to make myself new again. . . . Either I remake myself or I am done. I can't escape the dilemma longer. THAT is what has stopped me." To Laughlin he writes of the work's being given over to the critics, "I hope it cuts their hearts out. It won't; they're too grooved in their protective tracks ever to turn aside to see the dulled world close about them—always whistling into the distance." To posterity he says of *Paterson*, "It called for a poetry such as I did not know, it was my duty to discover or make such a context on the 'thought.' " As indication that this new poetry and new self had emerged, Williams asked Laughlin early in 1946 to drop the Carlos from his signature and to publish him henceforth as "William Williams." Flossie's objections, however, ended this plan.

That the method Williams decides on is akin not to the "cubism" he used in the earlier version of the poem but to a synthetic cubism is made apparent more by his comments to Ralph Nash than by any explanation of the poem he expressly provides. Nash's article, "The Use of Prose in *Paterson*" (1953) had separated the poem's prose into three general categories: (1) newspaper clippings and factual data, directly transcribed; (2) authorial summaries of historical data, excerpted from old newspapers, local histories, etc.; and (3) personal letters. It had further classified the materials as prose of Contemporary or of Historical Fact. Nash had then gone on to note: "I mean this to stress their nature as blocks of material coming into the poem from outside . . . . [A] letter (or anything else) written by someone other than the poet brings into the poem something of an air of documentation. Irrelevancies and private allusions emphasize that this is not exactly a piece of the poem, but a piece of the poet's world." He had then concluded of the device, "No doubt Williams intends it partly as a forceful marriage of his poem's world with that world of reality from which he is fearful of divorcing himself."

This marriage is precisely the effect of synthetic cubism and its building art out into life space, and one can understand Williams' enthusiastic response: "When I read, or had read to me, your article on my use of prose in my poem, *Paterson*, I was left speechless . . . . You have penetrated to a secret source of whatever power I possess and it has frightened me. . . . I shall have to study the distinctions you make between your observation of what I have done, for it strikes me as on the whole so just and acute an observation of my style that I still can't believe it." Still, the "instinctual" nature which Williams stresses cannot be without some degree of "consciousness" if his letters to Gregory and Laughlin are to be believed.

What Williams seems to suggest as instinctual and valuable is Nash's having found integral the poem's prose rhythms: "You have spotted it in my insistence on the use of prose *within the poem itself* [Williams' italics] when I did not see the reasons so clearly and that's why I think it so remarkable." This has particular reference to Nash's finding in the relationship of prose and poetry a meaningful kind of counterpoint: "It is evident that the prose affects the poem most strongly by its sound, by the inevitable interruption to eye and ear whenever one of the prose passages appears. This means, for one thing, that the prose is of tremendous importance to the pace and tempo of the entire poem. Nowhere is this more striking than in the eight pages of closely set type that provide a tortured, involved, garrulous, intimate, but ultimately dignified and quiet close for Book Two." Earlier Williams had written Parker Tyler (1948): "All the prose [in *Paterson*], including the tail which would have liked to have wagged the dog, has primarily the purpose of giving a metrical meaning to or of emphasizing a metrical continuity between all word use. It is *not* an antipoetic device . . . . It *is* that prose and verse are both *writing*, both a matter of the words and an interrelation between words for the purpose of exposition, or other better defined purpose of *the art*." Williams then asserts, "Poetry does not *have* to be kept away from prose as Mr. Eliot might insist, it goes *along with* prose and, companionably, by itself, without aid or excuse or need for separation or bolstering, shows itself by *itself* for what it is."

That Williams should express gratitude to Nash for his "discovery" may result from Randall Jarrell's attitude toward the poem which increasingly began to dismiss Williams' use of prose as capricious. In "A View of Three Poets" (1951), Jarrell had written: "It is interesting to see how much some later parts of *Paterson* resemble in their structure some middle and later parts of the *Cantos:* the Organization of Irrelevance (or, perhaps, the Irrelevance of Organization) suggests itself as a name for this

category of structure. Such organization is *ex post facto* organization: if something is somewhere, one can always find Some Good
Reason for its being there, but if it had not been there . . . would
one reader have guessed where it should have 'really' gone?" Jarrell
concludes that Chance is "sole arbiter" of the work. Even Robert
Lowell, who praises Book II of *Paterson* in the *Nation* (1948), was
compelled to refer to its "chunks of prose" as "raw" though, in an
especially apt comparison, he senses a kinship of the approach to
the use of factual material in the didactic chapters of Melville's
Moby-Dick.

However, both Jarrell and Lowell proceed from a concept of
unity in an art work which like the concept of unity in easel pictures was being supplanted. As Greenberg notes of the revolution
in "The Crisis of the Easel Picture" (1948), "The easel picture
subordinates decorative to dramatic effect. It cuts the illusion of
a box-like cavity into the wall behind it, and within this, as a
unity, it organizes three-dimensional semblances. To the extent
that the artist flattens out the cavity for the sake of decorative
patterning and organizes its contents in terms of flatness and
frontality, the essence of the easel picture—which is not the same
as its quality—is on the way to being compromised." The very
building out of synthetic cubism requires a new kind of expectation on the part of the viewer and hence a new kind of unity.

Although Williams disagreed generally with T. S. Eliot, he
seems in his statement about needing to remake himself to suggest
a closeness to Eliot's statement on Shakespeare in "John Ford"
(1932): "The whole of Shakespeare's work is *one* poem . . . . A
man might, hypothetically, compose any number of fine passages
or even of whole poems which would each give satisfaction, and
yet not be a great poet, unless we felt them to be united by one
significant, consistent, and developing personality." For Williams,
who appends John Addington Symonds' elucidation of the practice
of Hipponax to the opening book of the poem, the unity of *Paterson* might lie in its integration with his own personality, as in his
earlier poems the recurrent myth of Kora had suggested a relationship of those descents and returns and a psychological need
"to gather the assets of the whole personality together" into the
form of a personified thought at moments of despair and spatial
closure "and with this united strength to fling open the door of
the future." Indicating that the presence of Book V is a denial
of the internal unity of *Paterson's* first four books, Walter Sutton
in "Dr. Williams' *Paterson* and the Quest for Form" (1960) comes

to a like position: "The search for form and the quest for identity
are the same. Neither the city, the poet, nor the poem is a self-
sufficient entity. They are interdependent elements of a cultural
complex, and the definition of any one involves interaction." Sutton cites in support a statement in *I Wanted to Write a Poem*
(1958) where Williams indicates that *Paterson V* is needed not
because he feels some organic lack but because *he* no longer
believes that death ends anything. But Sutton might also have
cited the lines in Book III of *Paterson* where Williams speaks
paradoxically of the clarity of the blurring "between man and /
his writing" so one is no longer certain "as to which is the man
and / which the thing and of them both which / is the more to
be valued."

One suspects that the marvelling which Williams does in Nash's
"ex post facto organization" comes precisely because he had rejected this avenue of a unity within the work as an avenue of
understanding. Indication of this is provided in his letter to
Norman Macleod (1945). Fearing that *Paterson* might not be
accepted "because of its formlessness," Williams had written:
"Christ! Are there no intelligent men left in the world? Dewey
might do something for me, but I am not worth his notice." The
reference is undoubtedly to John Dewey's extension of the James-
ian "stream of consciousness" into "contexts of experience." These
"contexts" saw the continuity of life as a gradation of qualitative
fusions, here and there broken into by articulated analyses and
discriminations. Unity in art became a system of fusions including
those with "fringe" elements outside the art work that existed so
long as a problematic situation did not arise to force breakage by
a discontinuous counter quality of discrimination or analysis. When
Nash was able to find counterpoint in the work, Williams could
feel more at ease that such a dominant quality of fusion did occur
and that his new poetics did not "destroy" the "unity" of the old,
much in the same way he could feel at ease with controlled measure, having felt, as he notes in "An Essay on *Leaves of Grass*"
(1955), that free verse was immoral.

The new poetics, as Greenberg was to relate it in art, had much
to do with altering illusion: "This tendency appears in the all-over,
'decentralized,' 'polyphonic' picture that relies on a surface knit
together of identical or closely similar elements which repeat
themselves without marked variation from one edge of the picture
to the other. It is a kind of picture that dispenses, apparently,
with beginning, middle, end. Though the 'all-over' picture will,
when successful, still hang dramatically on a wall, it comes very

close to decoration—to the kind seen in wallpaper that can be repeated indefinitely—and insofar as the 'all-over' picture remains an easel picture, which somehow it does, it infects the notion of the genre with a fatal ambiguity." The music terminology, Greenberg confesses, was borrowed advisedly from the work Kurt List and René Leibowitz had done on Schönberg's methods of composition, especially in light of Kahnweiler's earlier equivalencies between Gris's form of cubism and Schönberg's twelve-tone music.

Critics have been quick to note comparable musical and repetitive devices in *Paterson*, but in so doing, they have slighted the art connections. Jarrell, for example, in "The Poet and His Public" (1946) calls "the organization of *Paterson* . . . musical to an almost unprecedented degree: Dr. Williams introduces a theme that stands for an idea, repeats it over and over in varied forms, develops it side by side with two or three more themes that are being developed, recurs to it time and time again throughout the poem, and echoes it for ironic or grotesque effects in thoroughly incongruous contexts." Thomas R. Whitaker in *William Carlos Williams* (1968) goes so far as to deny the metaphor of art: "In trying to elucidate . . . we may be tempted to discuss the poem as a mosaic or as some other spatial form. But to do so would be to lose sight of its temporal core. And even a musical analogy, which may enable us to talk about its orchestration of themes, cannot fully cope with its existential mode of progression." Greenberg concludes his discussion of the crisis of the easel picture by returning, like Williams, to personality as a final arbiter of structure: "The dissolution of the pictorial into sheer texture, into apparently sheer sensation, into an accumulation of repetitions, seems to speak for and answer something profound in contemporary sensibility."

But none of these issues resolves finally the issues of dimensionality in *Paterson*, though they provide a sounder basis for one's discussion of it. The dimensionality of synthetic cubism which does intrude on actual life space is still different from the dimensionality of a poem which, however modified, remains a system of illusions, none of which in the end leaves the actual dimensions of the printed page. Thus the intrusion of art into the life space of the reader is, in effect, a psychological intrusion predicated upon a separation which is made mentally between fact and fiction, and it is this psychological separation which Williams is attacking. For Williams, as he reiterated time and again, both are parts of the one cyclical process of descent and return, and through both life may be lived more fully. Previously he had kept the two separate enough that life might be illuminated by art and art by life. Book

I of *Paterson,* which opens with a colon and closes with a statement about the interrelatedness of art and life, ends this clear
separation. The colon usually indicates that what follows is an
explanation, a list, an enumeration connected to what has preceded. Here what has preceded is clearly life, and thus, from the
very onset, with the statement of the poem's *"plan for action to
supplant a plan for action"* to the book's end, in an espousal of
what Yvor Winters would call "the fallacy of imitative form," an
assault on a separation of art and life occurs. Within this larger
assault lie the smaller battles of fact and fiction, male and female,
past and present, one and many, and marriage and divorce.

Yet these assaults, as the work's overriding themes of divorce
and blockage connote, take place in facet-planes whose "interpenetration, both ways" is meant to result in rest, hopefully the "picture of perfect rest" defined by Williams in *Kora* as the basis of
permanence in art. Their equal bidirectional stresses lie open not
to the psychological descents and returns of Williams' early poetry
but to the illusions of eternality which characterize his Objectivist
poetics. As one cannot progress in and out of blockage, the "hope-
less and desperate situations" which had moved Williams in these
early poems from life into art and then back into life or from
present into past and then back into present, become here merely
decorative. The increasingly mechanical coherence of their ma-
chined contours and ornamentally raw prose segments and the
heraldic, suspended clusters of signs and lyrics through which
the reader moves suggest a designer's rather than a poet's world.
The lateral movements defined by sequence, spatial metaphors,
parallelism, and repetition may reveal the intrinsic relationships
of the parts but the reader cannot say that anything "human" is
rescued from the arrangement. The image of death which ends
Book IV and from which the young poet and the swimmer spring
as a new beginning does not so much conclude the poem as confirm
its preoccupation with continuity, suggested by its title Pater-son
and its closing image of the hanged John John-son. But this
continuity, as Williams reveals in "Letter to an Australian Editor"
(1946), is not male to male. It does not reside in "the assumption
that it was mind that fertilizes mind" and in a cutting of one's
self "from that supplying female" (society), but in a renewal of
"the close tie between the poet and the upsurging (or down surg-
ing) forms of his immediate world." This "close tie," as even he
forgot by the close of Book IV, is negated by a prophecy of return
whose immediacy, like the prophecy of spring at the beginning of

"A Coronal," can only be suggested. Thus, unlike the ends of Books I and II, which could bring a reader back into life, or "A Coronal," which did carry the reader into spring, Book IV can only bring him into a vision not of an immediate world but of future life. The futurity of this vision may well be the price of the work's blurring of life and art. Where else but the future can it be resolved since the very blurring eliminates the present and past as possibilities? In any case, the failure of the poem to move back into an immediate world prevents any psychological affirmations like those which resolve his early poems.

In "William Carlos Williams' *Paterson*" (1965), Richard Gustafson proposes that the repetitions are designed to "show the various ways by which man tries to unlock his mind to find beauty"— dead history, self-indulgence, books, the future, and finally art, but, whereas one might concede that these themes like their corresponding metaphors of man (the Passaic Falls), woman (the Park), artificial man (the city), and artificial woman (society) are phenomenologically right in their outward movement, they are mechanical in that the blockage which Williams depicts prevents any smooth outward flow. Yet a poem about blockage whose operative mode conveys facility would defeat the theme as a semanticist's 300-page manuscript about man's inability to communicate somehow defeats by an underlying hope of communication its own basic premise. One feels that rather than blockage Williams would have been wiser to center his poem on the theme of difficult passage. Nevertheless, one should not assume that the failure of *Paterson's* overall design negates it as a significant production or precludes the successes of many of its parts. As in much Romantic poetry, the failed long poem becomes a vehicle for a series of small lyrical successes, and often in the work's course, the reader comes across powerful and exquisite sections.

Nor should one let the failures of dimensionality and descent obscure the fact of the poem's conscious and innovative use of cubism. Like Gris, who proposed to move from cylinders to particular bottles, Williams announces early in Book I that he will move "from mathematics to particulars," and the structural device of facet-planes constructed like those of "To a Solitary Disciple" by breaks and parallelism is clear. Moreover, the warp and woof which Williams identifies as another characteristic of cubism is clearly these particulars being played against the image of the falls. As Sister Bernetta Quinn indicates in "*Paterson:* Listening to Landscape" (1970), Williams in one tentative beginning encircled with heavy blue crayon the sentence: "It is the FALLS, continuously falling; use it as background to everything else, to heighten everything else and to stitch together every other thing." He also marked the passage at the side with red crayon. The plan which Williams summarized for readers when Book III appeared (1949) reaffirms this intention: "From the beginning I decided there would be four books following the course of the river whose life seemed more and more to resemble my own life as I more and more thought of it: the river above the Falls, the catastrophe of the Falls itself, the river below the Falls, and the entrance at the end into the great sea." Various critics have spotted the connection of this river with the mind's stream of consciousness, making this concept of the flow of thought ultimately the abstract, architectural strands with which the individual lines will interlace. Support for their identification may be found both within *Paterson* and in "The Mind Hesitant" (1948), where Williams admits: "Sometimes the river / becomes a river in the mind / or of the mind / or in and of the mind." Earlier in "The Poet of *Paterson Book One*" (1946), Parker Tyler had suggested the river's connection with the Liffey and James Joyce's *Finnegans Wake* and Sister Bernetta Quinn in her essay offers an additional connection with the Don and Mikhail Sholokhov's *And Quiet Flows the Don.* Lastly, the "cubist" solidification of language is apparent in Williams' going out into life and introducing "life" language into "literary" language. This is evinced in his using letters, newspaper accounts, documents, histories, and other clearly non-illustrious aids to strengthen the illusion of art and life intermingling. It is also supported by the belief, noted in his *Autobiography*, that "in the very lay of the syllables 'Paterson'" he intended not God but Paterson to be discovered.

What the failures of dimensionality and descent do suggest about *Paterson* and its attempts to use cubism is a confirmation of Pound's feeling in "Dr. Williams' Position" (1928) that if Williams ever used form he would use it *ab exteriore* and that when "plot, major form, or outline" are "put on *ab exteriore*, they probably lead only to dullness, confusion or remplissage or the 'falling between two stools.'" *Paterson's* design clearly removes it from the immediacy and urgency of Williams' lyrics, but as clearly it is not a lyric poem. At best, it is, as Roy Harvey Pearce suggests in *The Continuity of American Poetry* (1961), a lyric-epic. As a lyric-epic it uses the platform space created by its own prophecy as a locus from which to observe the present conforming to a prescribed plan. The voyeurism which this vantage point makes possible, different in kind from that suggested in his *Autobiography* by his observations of patients, provides him with the psychic distance which Joyce in *A Portrait of the Artist as a Young Man* (1916) makes essential to the epical form. It provides the center of an emotional gravity which is equidistant from the artist himself and from others, but without the prolonged brooding upon himself that Joyce defines as the method of such distancing. Williams' lyrics which were predicated, like Joyce's definition of the form, upon the "simplest verbal vesture of an instant of emotion" resisted by their very nature, a structure, even prophecy, imposed from the outside. These early poems as a consequence carried in their realizations clear unconscious patterns, and one feels that these unconscious patterns provided them in part with much of their strength. When Williams uses conscious patterns as he does in *Paterson* and even to a degree in "Asphodel, That Greeny Flower" (1954), one cannot help feeling a lessening or diverting of this strength.

Peter Meinke

William Carlos Williams.
Traditional Rebel

William Carlos Williams is more and more recognized as supplanting Eliot and Pound as an influence on American poetry. His directness, flat idiom, clear "objective" imagery can be found in the poems of Theodore Roethke, Denise Levertov, Gary Snyder, and most of the "new poets," and I believe he has also had a modifying effect on such major "academic" poets as Howard Nemerov, Robert Lowell, and John Berryman, pushing their lines toward a greater simplicity, a more homely diction. What is less recognized is that Williams uses many traditional devices in his

From *Mad River Review,* II (Winter-Spring 1967), 57-64. Reprinted by permission of the journal.

poetry, that despite all his "newness" he is still in the major English lyric tradition, representing the apotheosis of the Romantic tenets of organic form, spontaneity as opposed to cerebration, and the language of the common man; he is, in short, a traditional rebel.

Williams' own critical language, his "triadic stanza" and "variable foot," only tends to confuse the picture; his poetic technique can be much more easily explained with such traditional terms as alliteration, rhyme, stanzaic and sound patterns. Certainly there is great variation in his style; just as certainly there is a *general* uniformity in the way his poems are put together. For example, when Williams writes the first stanza of a poem, the following stanzas will have the same number of lines, a similar number of accents in the equivalent lines, even approximately the same shape on the page: his verse is far from "free." In fact, in some of his long poems such as "Asphodel, That Greeny Flower," what we have is a sort of *revivication by rearrangement* of the rhythms of blank verse:

> I have to say to you
> and you alone
> but it must wait
> while I drink in
> the joy of your approach . . .

or,

> Honeysuckle! And now
> there comes the buzzing of a bee!
> and a whole flood
> of sister memories. . . .

He easily incorporates Spenser's iambics into the structure:

> "Sweet Thames, run softly
> till I end
> my song,"

But a more typical Williams' arrangement can be found by analyzing his short poems. I've chosen, more or less at random, the first poem in *Pictures from Brueghel*, "Self-Portrait," but the same technique can be used on the majority of Williams' poems, from

his famous "Red Wheelbarrow" to many sections of *Paterson*.[1]
Here is "Self-Portrait":

> In a red winter hat blue
> eyes smiling
> just the head and shoulders
>
> crowded on the canvas
> arms folded one
> big ear the right showing
>
> the face slightly tilted
> a heavy wool coat
> with broad buttons
>
> gathered at the neck reveals
> a bulbous nose
> but the eyes are red-rimmed
>
> from over-use he must have
> driven them hard
> but the delicate wrists
>
> show him to have been a
> man used to
> manual labor unshaved his
>
> blond beard half trimmed
> no time for any-
> thing but his painting

First of all, this is clearly a Williams' poem: the lack of punctuation, the disarming simplicity, the *sound* of the words, the nervous rhythm; we recognize it immediately. The question is, How
does it work? Why is it "good"? To find out, we must take up
these points individually.

Writing a poem without punctuation does several things. It puts
an extremely heavy weight on the structure and on the order of
the words; it gives an open-ended tension, an all-at-once-ness that
keeps the parts suspended in the air; it emphasizes the oral aspect
of the poem; it make certain words (like "smiling") ambiguous,
adding to the overall tension. The poem consists of 21 short lines

---

[1]William Carlos Williams, *Pictures From Brueghel* (New Directions, 1963),
p. 3.

divided into seven 3-line stanzas, with the second line in each stanza being the shortest in each case, at least visually. As has been noted often, Williams' poetry has strong affinities with painting, especially cubist painting, and he puts great care into the way a poem looks on the page (looks *and* sounds, the total organism); with this kind of control, he does not need punctuation. His poems *are*, in a sense, pictures.

The lack of punctuation also underlines any punctuation mark he might use, strikingly so in the poem's last stanza, where we find the hyphen after "any" (the only other punctuation marks being part of the actual spelling of a word, as in "red-rimmed"). Why not write:

> blond beard half trimmed
> no time for anything
> but his painting   . . . . ?

Williams *can't* write it this way because it would break up the visual pattern of the poem (making the last line shorter); hyphenating also emphasizes the important part of the word ("any-") and contributes to the "zippy-zappy" rhythm, to use a fine Williams' word. A poet's job is to refresh his language, and Williams does this over and over by this breaking up of components (as he does in, say, "a red wheel / barrow"). Again, if he had not hyphenated "any- / thing" the poem would have had a much more conclusive final rhythm which would work against the unresolved chord he strives for. And, as we will see, he needed to make two words of "anything" to satisfy his desire for precision.

The disarming simplicity of Williams' poetry is the result of several things: a generally simple "unpoetic" vocabulary, which makes certain words leap out in contrast; a peculiar directness of approach, as if hurrying to tell us everything (helped by lack of punctuation); and an almost breathless urgency of tone. In "Self-Portrait" the simple vocabulary is made particularly effective by an almost mathematical device: "bulbous," the only word that is at all "poetic," is used as a hinge in the exact center of the poem, in the middle of the middle line of the middle stanza (there are even 42 words preceding it and 42 words following it—counting "any- / thing" as two: *that's* control!). This is an interesting means of composition, but how does one justify this positioning, that is, is it more than a poetic whimsey? For one thing, this form suits the content, the bulbous nose centering both Brueghel's

portrait and Williams' poem: Williams begins with the hat and
ends with the beard, placing the nose appropriately in the middle.
Williams uses "bulbous" instead of the more colloquial "swollen"
to call attention to this structure. He also, of course, uses it for
the sound, which I'll deal with later.

Williams' "simplicity" (which I hope I'm showing is not so
simple) is aided by his directness. This is especially evident when
one compares Williams' Brueghel poems with Auden's "Musée
des Beaux Arts" or Berryman's "Winter Landscape." Williams'
poems on the same pictures do not have the overt statements on
history and philosophy found in the others; this is true also of
"Self-Portrait." He gets this directness partially through lack of
grammar: there is nothing that can be thought of as a complete
sentence until line 8, and because there is no punctuation even
this is ambiguous. It is as if he has no time for the niceties, but
must hurry to communicate, to *re-create*, Brueghel's portrait to
us. Howard Nemerov's fine poem "Vermeer" embraces Williams'
philosophy or practice very nicely:

> If I could say to you, and make it stick,
> A girl in a red hat, a woman in blue
> Reading a letter, a lady weighing gold . . .
> If I could say this to you so you saw,
> And knew, and agreed that this was how it was
> In a lost city across the sea of years,
> I think we should be for one moment happy. . . .

This hurried air is particularly appropriate for "Self-Portrait"
because it suits the subject so well: "no time for any- / thing but
his painting"; Williams wants us to feel this in the very structure
and grammar of the poem. Like a good painter, he seeks both
immediacy and timelessness with the whole of his composition. All
of this is intensified by a typical Williams' device: he implies an
urgency of action which he does not explain. *So much depends*
on a red wheelbarrow or (in "Asphodel") "I have to say to you /
and you alone." Here, he underlines the drive of the painter:

> but the eyes red-rimmed
> from over-use he must have
> driven them hard

He does not say *why* he must have driven them hard: this is left
up to the reader and adds greatly to the over-all tension of the

poem. He is implying, of course, the *urgency* of all art, his own included.

A major element in the composition of any Williams' poem is the sound. I feel that he generally puts sounds together in a musical way (despite his misleading "flatness"); that is, he tends to cluster related sounds together, as a musician uses related notes. For example, in his famous poem on plums he isolates such sound-related words as "icebox," "breakfast," "delicious"; in the red wheelbarrow poem we find "glazed with rain" and "beside the white." Because Williams usually uses few words, their sounds assume a particular importance.

The large role of alliteration in his poetry is generally overlooked. We have several examples in "Self-Portrait" but the main alliterative letter is "b" (there are "b's" in each stanza): this is why he writes "bulbous" instead of "swollen." "Bulbous" picks up the preceding "broad buttons" and the following "blond beard" as well as the two "buts" and a "big" that lead off their respective lines, and the "blue" that ends the first line. We also have "crowded on canvas" and "red-rimmed" as further alliteration, as well as "neck" and "nose," and "slightly tilted." There are, too, related words emphasized in alternate lines: "must," "wrists," "unused."

Williams uses rhyme more than most critics realize, because he mutes it by using it irregularly, generally internally. In this poem we find only "red" and "head," but rhyme is to be found over and over in his poems. A more common device is the juxtaposition of words that *almost* rhyme: half-rhymes and "slant" rhymes. In "Self-Portrait" "shoulders," "folded," "showing," "coat," "nose" follow in short succession; we also find "right" and "slightly," "labor unshaved," "unused to manual," "trimmed" and "time," "any-thing" and "painting," and others. When one considers that all these relationships occur within just 85 words, one can see the care and skill that have gone into the construction of these sound-patterns. It is not "smoothly" lyrical any more than Brueghel's paintings are "pretty," but "Self-Portrait" is composed more musically than most so-called lyrics.

The last distinguishing trait of a Williams' poem that I want to discuss is the nervous rhythm of the lines and the effect this produces. We all recognize the opening lines as having a typical Williams' "feel":

> In a red winter hat blue
> eyes smiling

Why is it better the way Williams has it than the more conventional order of:

> In a red winter hat
> blue eyes smiling . . . ?

First, if poetry is to "make it new, make it strange," Williams' order accomplishes this; but that's too easy and can justify almost anything. Williams' arrangement is good for *specific* reasons of sound, sight, sense, and rhythm. The position of "blue" emphasizes the first "b" sound which builds to the later alliteration; the sight keeps it to the visual pattern of the poem; the splitting of "blue" and "eyes" creates a tension and an ambiguity of grammar (maybe "eyes" and "smiling" should also be split—it sets the tone), and the linking of "red" and "blue" in the same line reminds us that this is a poem about a painting: Williams uses words as an artist uses colors; and finally, this particular grouping of words forces us into that herky-jerky rhythm that keeps us off balance, pulling us backwards and forwards on the wire of Williams' lines. Where we expect, in common speech, to stop, Williams forces us to go on; where we expect to go on, he forces us to stop:

> arms folded one
> big ear the right showing

We are constantly surprised, right to the end:

> no time for any-
> thing but his painting

The break trips us, rhythmically and linguistically, then rushes us forward to the end where we are left dangling. Where most poems try to build up to an impressive climax, Williams' poems begin and end abruptly, slices of life without the final comment. He could write the other way, as in his skillful "The Yachts," but "The Yachts," though good, is not typical of Williams.

One could write considerably more on "Self-Portrait," but I

hope I've done enough to show how careful a craftsman Williams was. It doesn't matter if he did it all consciously or unconsciously (though it's clear that *most* of it was done consciously). It seems to me that what most of Williams' disciples and imitators lack is his craftsmanship; they see Williams as a rebel who brought the breath of freedom into poetry. What they don't see is his tremendous mastery of traditional poetic devices used in a refreshing way. Poetry is an art and a discipline: the closer one looks at Williams' poems, the more one admires the discipline of his art.

Hugh Kenner

William Carlos Williams: In Memoriam

His innocence lingers: innocence and aching vulnerability. He went unprotected by any public role. He wouldn't have known how to be a literary man if he had wanted to try. One day he read from his poems, for an hour or so, in (wasn't it?) a Newark department store, more or less heard, one imagines, by holiday shoppers. He would have been seventy-five then, and he did it because he was invited to. (Who could have invited him? The management?) He believed fiercely in poems, in a public need for words released, set dancing: he would do anything at all to serve that belief.

> . . . Look at
> what passes for the new
> You will not find it there but in
> despised poems.
> It is difficult
> to get the news from poems

From *National Review,* XIV (1963), 237. Reprinted by permission of the journal.

> yet men die miserably every day
> for lack
> of what is found there. . . .

Yet so disengaged was he from his own achievement that he died, six months short of his eightieth birthday, pathetically unpersuaded of its magnitude. It was the only pathetic trait in an indomitable man.

For no role sustained him. Has any poet ever before rejected so radically the stay, and temptation, of poet's status? It was a heroic venture, persisted in for six decades. Williams struck a miraculous equilibrium: he did a job as a poet, and with such passion and tenacity that American poetry groups itself around twin peaks, Williams and Whitman; but as to what he *was*, he was a physician. The careers twinned from the start.

He had the physician's toughness, the physician's irritability. He had his sleep broken too often by nuisance house-calls to cosset his medical life in sentimentalities. All those people whom he served with passion upheld him and encroached on him. He had stood by too often at needless deaths to believe in either the infallible power of man to intervene, or in the capacity of merely conventional words to sustain. The bereaved long for words, the dying long to speak them. It is when we try to speak from the heart that we understand how man's way is smoothed by ritual, and regret the deadness of our residual rituals in a pragmatic time.

The pathetic verse whose neck Williams saw no point in wringing, the limp iambic rhymes that struggled up toward heaven in 1910 out of every opened magazine in New Jersey, constituted a dead residual ritual, pointless, offensive. He set out to carry American verse in one lifetime, by sheer intensity of application, all the way from demotic speech to indigenous ceremony: "a reply to Greek and Latin with the bare hands."

Every day in his consulting room people struggled and stammered, the illiterate people as well as the normally glib, to convey the simplest matters, matters justifying an often difficult journey to an interview that would have to be paid for: my child's pallor, my aching foot, and the meaning of these facts in worry and disequilibrium.

No poet has had a better chance to know how people are lost when they set about examining their lives, or to listen to American speech rhythms under stress. He wanted speech to issue as

though unpremeditated, word after word to drop into place: the
bare truth to sing.

> Let the snake wait under
> his weed
> and the writing
> be of words, slow and quick, sharp
> to strike, quiet to wait,
> sleepless.

> —through metaphor to reconcile
> the people and the stones.
> Compose. (No ideas
> but in things) Invent!
> Saxifrage is my flower that splits
> the rocks.

As the professional golfer can count on sinking a ten-foot putt
at one stroke, so years of tireless practice permitted him, sometimes, to write in fifteen minutes a poem as durable as the language can conceive. Those were the quarter-hours he lived for.
In old age, crippled by stroke after stroke, his speech impaired,
his right hand paralyzed, he would still sit early of a morning at
his electric typewriter, dropping the maneuvered finger on one key
after another, writing and rewriting sometimes brief sketches,
sometimes very long poems. The fifth part of *Paterson*, the great
meditation on love and on his own death ("Asphodel, That Greeny
Flower"), the whole of the work contained in *Pictures from Brueghel*, came out of those years.

Language and the Poet

A lifetime's discipline raised up, out of the pain and plodding
and confusion of those last mornings, an effortless artless elo-
quence, as tender or as vigorous as he could want it to be: as
though he had been schooling himself all his life for the time
when he would have his freest work to do, and would have to do
it under those conditions. The first four books of *Paterson* (1946-
51) are his most solid achievement; the last work (*Pictures from
Brueghel*, 1962) the most poignant, simplest and loveliest. He
had brought the language by concern and love to an utter, feminine responsiveness. He wrote often about the language itself, and
about the imagination's way with it: never better than in the

"Song" he conceived one morning with Botticelli's Venus somewhere in his limpid, eager mind, and saw printed in this magazine two years ago:

> beauty is a shell
> from the sea
> where she rules triumphant
> till love has had its way with her
>
> scallops and
> lion's paws
> Sculptured to the
> tune of retreating waves
>
> undying accents
> repeated till
> the ear and the eye lie
> down together in the same bed